THE BABY

WRESTLER

The Secret Life of A Happy SAHD

By

James Cyril McGowan

For A.M.

Contents

Preface: Earnestness for the Disbelieving 9

The Baffled King 14

The Harrowing 22

Robinson Crusoe on Venus 32

Koyaanisqatsi 36

Why Not Stay At Home? 40

Rude Baptisms on a Blue Planet 44

Our First Son Wore a Dog Suit 49

Ode to Needy Angels 56

The Milk-Plus Bar 61

A Moveable Feast 66

In Praise of Fair to Middling Babysitters 71

Here In Zombie Land 74

Get Out of My Office 81

The Look that Knows Better 85

Do What I Say And Nobody Gets Hurt 89

To Sleep and Sleep Not 95

My Kryptonite 98

The Big T 103

What Did You Do In The War, Daddy? 107

The Big E 114

Father Time 118

Another Supposedly Helpful Thing I'll Never Do
Again 123

The Ethics of Elfland 132

Sunday Morning Sleeping-In.................. 140

Where's Dada? 140

Meditations in an Emergency................. 145

The Wild Kingdom.................................. 152

Dance Dance Revolution 158

The Year of Plumbing Dangerously........ 161

Burnin' Down the House!........................ 164

Let's Roll.. 167

Doctors, Dentists, Barbers, and Blog-based Business
Promoters 170

The Things They Carried........................ 173

Our Mothers... 175

Our Fathers 178

A Modest Proposal................................. 182

Tears, Inconvenience, God, and Poetry... 189

A Fairy Tale of New York........................ 195

You Have No Idea 198

8 ½ 207

The Three Amigos 212

Attack of the Indigo Children.................. 217

Rabid Sports Fans.................................. 220

Little Women 226

Great Expectations 231

The Used Couch that Sent Me to Italy 235

Things Fall Apart 249

The Divine Comedy 255

Unwrapping the Present 258

The Primary Love Object 263

It is All Over. It Has Just Begun 268

False Endings 271

Preface: Earnestness for the Disbelieving

In buying this book, you have invested hard-earned money in the search for easy answers to the dilemma of how to raise perfect children. As proof that you have made the right decision, I hereby offer you an exclusive money-back guarantee that models of perfection shall be delivered unto you simply by putting my words into action. Your offspring will cheerfully obey your every command, attend Ivy League schools, pair up with perfect mates, and care for you lovingly in your old age. You can now dispense with all the other child-rearing volumes that imply such outcomes. After all, do you really want to put your future at risk, not to mention your children's future, and by extension, the very future of civilization by employing methods that fail to offer an explicit guarantee? Herein, you have it. Now please allow me to elaborate on the winding road that led me to the revelations you so desperately seek.

My name is Jim, and I'm a recovering Stay-At-Home-Dad (SAHD). I admit that I'm powerless over children. The experience of almost single-handedly caring for multiple little people has pruned back my neural tree to the point where it now resembles a shrubbery overly favored by the family dog. But I pledge to regain a serious view of myself, and of the society that we grown-ups have created. I began writing this report in order to give voice to the 3 million other desperate SAHDs out there, whose silent sufferings go unreported by Amnesty International. However, soon after engaging the task, I had an epiphany: if just ten percent of the SAHD population buys it, I would be able to hire a nanny, perhaps even a blonde one from Sweden, and return to the adult world where I could once again indulge in all its cravings for money, power, celebrity, exclusive entertainment, fine dining and luxurious bedding. A successful book would put me back on the fast track toward all of those false gods, as well as any others that might pop into my reduced field of consciousness. Only with the help of my higher power, coupled with your monetary assistance, do I stand a chance of reclaiming the desires proper to my birthright as a red-blooded American male, which I misplaced somewhere amidst the multicolored plastic clutter of modern childhood. Still, I am aware that I must take it one day at a time.

I also confess that I am tired of being a mutant, a biogenetic experiment cut loose in a hostile environment to see if there are any benefits. Science has shown that ever since our species was crawling amongst the high branches, it's been the females who carried the babies riding atop their backs or clinging to their chests. It was the women who spent their lives raising little people up to become bigger ones. It was the women who managed the food input/output system, amongst other frivolous duties involving continuance of the human race. If you're a man who takes up these jobs and dares to reverse the sacred order of nature, you will find yourself a fish out of water equipped with only very stubby fins that you must use to crawl through the mud. Whether the caretaking gene that switched on somewhere in the recesses of my DNA will prove the death of me, or the spark of a beneficial adaptation, is unfolding now in real time. A firm answer as to whether it will be beneficial to the overall species probably lies several generations into the future. For now, I must persevere across the muddy plain, gasping for oxygen, blinking in the bright sunlight, and hoping to God that my mate is wrong about the possibility that this path is taking a toll on my sanity.

Which brings me to survival of the fittest from a proto-capitalist, marketing point of view. If you bought this book, the mutation represents one of evolution's success stories, but if you borrowed it from a friend, it isn't, unless you recommend it to someone with the money to buy a copy. Like all evolutionary theory, things get tricky rather quickly. Maybe you're borrowing this book from a library, which is okay since the library bought a copy, but it also means that you're cheap, like me, and I can rule out your buying a SAHD action figure from which I can expect merchandising royalties. If by some miracle this book does make money, the wild gene of male caretaking set loose in our capitalist system might touch off a global revolution that changes the course of history, or maybe just give me a decent shot at paying the piano teacher. Either way, let me remind you that you shall get your perfect kids as long as you keep reading the following passages. Furthermore, if you encourage others to buy this book, you shall eventually live in a world filled with perfect people. So please consider yourself to be an official sponsor of Utopia. Congratulations!

Now for some housekeeping; a term with which I have become all-too familiar, as you will too, if you choose to "tune in, turn on, and drop out." Marshall McLuhan was not referring to television, drugs, or leaving school when he came up with that saying. He meant something far deeper and much more subversive. Dedicated SAHDs and MAHDs (Mothers at Home Disenfranchised) are among the few people currently trying to live by his words. Old Marshall hovers over some of the following chapters like a patron saint because his predictions about our media saturated society are finally hitting home, with our children being the biggest casualties. He would approve of this book's form, which follows its function. I wrote the short missives in great haste from the front lines. If you're doing the same work that I am, then you too will live by the three-sentence rule: you will be allowed to neither read nor write more than three sentences without being interrupted by clarion calls such as "Daddy! Can you wipe me?"

If you are not currently engaged in this work, then you might find yourself feeling disoriented by the short chapters containing unvarnished factual accounts laid out with little apparent logic. I will have then successfully recreated in you exactly how it feels to be a SAHD. Children will turn your world upside down and then subvert your place in it, or vice-a-versa, with no warning. Things that you had previously thought were very important will suddenly appear ridiculous, while what had sounded absolutely ridiculous can become paramount. If you do choose to take them on, consider yourself forewarned: these tiny terrorists of love will never be satisfied until the old you has been demolished by any means necessary. There is no other way for them to turn out perfect. Guaranteed.

The Baffled King

*The first day of April is the day we remember what we are
the other 364 days of the year.*

Samuel Clemens

I was jolted out of one dream world and into another by the
heaving and hurling of our wolf-dog right beside the bed. Duke
was an extraordinarily beautiful golden animal, but the mélange
of sights, sounds, and smells that he was creating at that moment
forever secured his place in the pantheon of artists of repulsion. I
had no choice but to bolt from the covers into the predawn
winter darkness, grab him by the collar and hustle him
downstairs toward the front door. The commotion woke both
kids, who began wailing like Banshees. The moment I got Duke
outside onto the frozen ground where he could express himself

with abandon, he decided that he was finished throwing up. His installation was site-specific to my bedroom.

I turned and rushed back upstairs to face the high-decibel sonic assault coming at me from all quarters. Girl was standing in her crib with her sleeper sagging under the weight of a wet brown mess that had blown out through both leg holes. Boy was screaming even louder because he was not to be out-done by her in anything. I swept Girl up and over to my satellite office, the changing table, where I spend so much time that I had installed a phone on the wall. One can conduct business while wrestling a squirming toddler out of her clothes and dirty diaper, but you will end up lathered in poop, and the piercing screams will prompt the party on the other end of the line to consider calling child protective services. I opened up the diaper, releasing the smells from hell, and began the all-important wiping process when the phone rang with perfect timing as usual.

A credit card representative with a superior sounding attitude informed me that I was two months overdue on a payment. The expense of moving from a rural town to the tri-State area had left me with astronomical balances on half a dozen cards that will take years to pay off. I was trying to be careful to pay them on time, but the warren of unpacked moving boxes that we called home had made the job of keeping track a bit complicated. I informed the agent that he was mistaken. All the bills were paid.

15

He then confirmed my address, which is not where I live at all, nor as it turns out, where anyone lives, because it's a place in Harrisburg that doesn't technically exist. An identity thief had changed the address on my credit files so that they could charge thousands of dollars in my name without my even knowing it. Although I had little cash, I managed to keep a good credit rating, which allowed my family to buy a home and procure the essentials. If a thief bombed my rating, things could get grim. Despite my pleas, the financial authorities who controlled my fiscal existence were now believing some stranger who was claiming to be me, while doubting that I was in fact me. The struggle for my identity against a doppleganger who appeared out of nowhere felt like some kind of weird out-of-body experience. It didn't help that my identity was already in flux due to my decision to leave the paid workforce and take on a job that's usually left to immigrant labor, but all of a sudden, things were becoming a bit too literal. The moment I hung up on that very strange call, the phone rang again.

This time it was the realtor, who said that she'd finally found an interested party for the house we'd been desperately trying to sell for the past eleven months. During those months, we were paying four mortgages: the first and second on the old house in Hershey, Pennsylvania, plus the first and second on the new one outside New York City. Our financial survival hinged on selling that old house yesterday. The realtor said I had to get the deed to the Hershey house to her right away, but that single sheet of paper was buried somewhere in boxes deeper than my old life, when I had been a global troubleshooter for the United Nations. The hubris generated by working for such a high-flying organization led me to believe that the tasks and annoyances of running a child-ridden household were safely within my range of competencies. I mean, how hard could they really be? It didn't yet occur to me that women might be superior to men in more than the obvious ways. At that moment, sunrise was breaking, the temperature was rising into the teens, and I still felt competent to deal with the situation.

The first thing you will discover on this job is that little children are certain that they were not meant to wear clothes. They will sabotage all your efforts to get them dressed, even when it's freezing outside, but never mind that for now. You must feed them first. The crying and screaming continued as they got locked into their high chairs. Food was shoveled into their mouths, alternatively by me and by their own bare hands. Thus occupied and restrained, they offered a few moments in which I could tear into the moving boxes in search of the missing deed. Home had also been my titular headquarters during the previous ten years while helping to build the Global Environment Facility from an idea into the world's largest environmental grant making machine, but the documents that had accumulated along the way were now thrown together with my personal papers into a whirlpool that threatened to suck me under. The clock was also ticking down to the time when my little Houdini would escape from his chair in the kitchen and either go for the butcher knives or the cellar stairs. By some miracle, I laid my hands on the deed amidst the rubble, and marveled at the amazing progress I was making over the day's hurdles.

Okay, everybody into the car for a rush trip to Fed-X. One of the benefits of being a man on this job is that I can carry two kids, one under each arm, against their will when they don't want to join me. Wait a minute! I forgot to clean up the dog chow reversal before the reek permeates the entire house. The task reminded me of my summer job as a teenager working for the New York City Housing Authority in the South Bronx. We'd clean squalid apartment complexes during the day that would magically become filthy again overnight. I recommend that work as excellent preparation for the job of child caretaker. The added challenge here is that you must somehow lock down little lunatics so that they don't do something life-threatening while you're attending to another pressing matter. But their mobility and intelligence increases by the minute, so what worked yesterday will not work today. You've got to be creative and stay ahead of the game. Good luck.

By now I've got the kids into their snowsuits and ready to go when the smell of another hugely dirty diaper permeates all those cold weather layers. Some frustration is building up, which in turn causes haste and results in hands fairly covered with toddler poop, which is no worse than dog vomit. Wait a minute though, could the combination spontaneously combust? I must live with that danger and hurry up because my 4 year-old boy has escaped outside into the snow.

I look up through the glass storm door to see that he's returned with a huge chunk of ice, which he hurls at the door, sending sheets of glass cascading into the house. Realtors, creditors, criminals, and miscreants are mounting a serious challenge to my mission of keeping our family from financial and physical ruin. I must forge ahead, tip-toeing over glass with toddler in arms so that I can buckle both kids into their car seats, entirely against their will once again. My key is in the ignition and I'm ready to go.

Click. Click. Click. No go. The battery is dead because boy turned on the interior light yesterday and it burned all night. I was going nowhere fast.

Meanwhile, the other me was barreling along the cyber-highway, unencumbered by kids, dogs, houses, or any of the other responsibilities that my real identity had accumulated. He had already changed all of the personal information on my credit file. People think I'm him when I call, and I can't convince them that

I'm actually me. I can't readily sell the old house or use credit cards or travel anywhere. Perhaps becoming me would be a fitting punishment for the poor sucker who wants my identity so badly. The joke would be entirely on him, because I'm already an imposter, a man trying to do a woman's job, and failing miserably at it. Since I'm the only person who believes that I am me anymore, I've begun to wonder about the real question here: who the hell am I?

I knew that I had been a professional who met with the Presidents from every country in North and South America all together in a big room while discussing a policy paper that I had written. I had reached the top of the game, and then chosen to go to the bottom, and been reborn as diaper man. Was I upside down, or was the world upside down? Even a six year-old boy could pick-up on my existential dilemma. He said, "Dad, did you ever wonder if you made the wrong decision? Wouldn't you rather be sharing an apartment with several scantily clad ladies?" This trenchant observation sent my mind into a momentary reverie, but I soon recovered and decided to tease out the errors that had landed me into this particular mess, and perhaps post them as a cautionary roadmap for others who might follow. The truth was that, like the poor souls in *The Nutty Professor* or *Dr. Jekyll and Mr. Hyde*, my identity was morphing radically and I had no idea who I was becoming. The only thing for certain was that a boy and a girl who carried my DNA were reengineering my mind relentlessly day and night. In a twist worthy of Dr. Frankenstein, my creations were also my agents of change. Perhaps the seeds of my downfall can be traced to their moments of creation, or at least to their moments of birth. For the sake of propriety, let us start with the latter.

The Harrowing

The poets who practice obstetrics and gynecology call it "turtling" when a baby's head peeks through the vagina, but then recedes back into the mysterious depths like a shy turtle on a quavering pond. Turtling is a deceptively peaceful term for what is actually a struggle to survive. The baby can be squeezed to death, or equally bad things can happen to the mother. There was no dispelling these grim realities from mind as I watched the doctors attach a large suction cup to our baby's head. One strong resident after another took turns trying to pull him out in a pitched tug-of-war that looked more like they were trying to land a record marlin than catch a little turtle. Exhaustion turned to vexation after eight doctors wore themselves out, and then began arguing whether to "take the baby" via Cesarean, or continue trying to extricate the turtle without killing it. While they debated about the best course of action, I began to seriously wonder whether fate was going to allow me to be a father, after all. The baby was right there—you could touch his head, but he was stuck in the doorway between life and death. I flashed on the first time that I had encountered that same liminal threshold, but during that episode, I had no time to pray.

As a teenager, the arc from competitive swimming to professional diving seemed like a natural progression. My hormone-addled brain was only capable of a sort of reduced logic—the kind that can conclude that since I had become supremely comfortable in the water, the aquatic realm would be a good place to make my living. The mental power to discern even basic contradictions was beyond me, like the fact that during swim racing you're completely free of cumbersome technology, while professional diving puts you into exactly the opposite position. The consequences of my limited perspective arrived one day while I was heading to the surface after doing some underwater welding. Just like prenatal babies, working divers use umbilical cords to supply them with air so that they can stay submerged for a full workday. My umbilical had become snagged on the bottom, stopping my ascent dead just a few feet from where the hydrosphere meets the atmosphere. Then, my helmet flooded. Looking upward, I could see sunlight dappling on the surface tantalizingly close. Everything beyond that point belonged to the world of the living, but I was trapped down in the world of the dead. I was either going to swim to the surface after extricating myself from the diving gear, which is normally requires two assistants while on the boat, or I was going to drown right then and there. The calm necessary to begin unbuckling the heavy harness descended upon me, and time slowed to a standstill. I was able to dump the gear and swim free to the surface. But I'd known workmates who found themselves in similar situations that did not turn out so well. Seeing their young faces at the funeral parlor sent me back to college pronto, and imbued me with a deep sense of the need to prioritize the important things during this brief life.

They decided to cut our first baby out of my wife's uterus just past midnight. The surgeon said that he found the boy swimming in a cesspool inside, because, it turns out, my wife's water had broken three days earlier. The young resident who examined her had sent us home, thinking that it hadn't. Wrong. Note to those pregnant: intrauterine infections grow quickly once the membrane gives way and the uterus is exposed to the outside environment.

They got Boy out of that mess, but he wouldn't take his crucial first breath. Wife looked up at me from the operating table and asked how he was doing, which was a simple question, really, except that they were frantically pumping air into his lungs with a black bag and the outcome was still up for grabs. It occurred to me that an honest assessment of the situation might not be the best thing to report to a woman whose uterus was sliced open and lying on her stomach with all its pink plumbing exposed. I hesitated to say anything, which made everything much worse because it caused her to imagine the very worst. My wife, A.M., is a medical researcher at a nonprofit foundation, but she is also an M.D., and during training, all M.D.s see their share of birthing horror stories. One can only imagine the scenarios replaying in her head as I stood there, dumbfounded and hoping for a miracle.

After what seemed like an eternity, the baby took a halting, wheezy breath, and they whisked him up to the neonatal ICU. My benumbed state of consciousness failed to register Strike One for my old life, which had blown right by me. I stood for a moment, stupefied in the wake of that hair-raising event, while one of Ernest Hemingway's early short stories swirled through my head. "Indian Camp" features a rural childbirth that's so excruciating and whose outcome is so uncertain that it drives the young Ojibway father who's listening in the next room to slit his own throat. Mother and child turn out fine, but in a wicked 180-degree twist from the usual disaster, the father dies. At the time I read it, I was an unmarried man with no inclination toward parenthood, and the story struck me as a little far-fetched. Not any more.

With only one child onboard, I could still fool myself into thinking that nothing would change. Life would go on as usual thanks to modern conveniences, take-out food, and young women who change diapers in exchange for hard currency. The term *working parent* has such a happily industrious, all-American ring to it that I adopted it without thought that the term might be totally meaningless. I don't know any *nonworking parents,* that is, unless you're in jail, dead, or have fled the family. But it was too soon to worry about that. The fact that my Wife had spent thirteen years in post-college education to work in an incredibly competitive field dedicated to the betterment of humankind wasn't about to change my hardwired concept of how households are run. I found a babysitter who stayed long hours while I traveled to New York or wherever the U.N. job took me because a man's place is out in the world.

Then a funny thing happened a year or so later on Father's Day. I was outside doing yard work when Wife came out onto the balcony, and tossed down a white plastic device that was bisected by an inscrutable blue line, heralding a surprising victory over birth control technology. We were expecting more company. That line would also separate my life into the old and the new, never mind that the old me was a younger man, and the new me a much older one. I was smugly convinced that there was no way I was going to let a little thing like having another baby in the house change my way of life in the slightest. Our babysitter would be happy to take on another in-house client.

Wife grew concerned that I might not survive another one of her attempts at vaginal childbirth, so she scheduled a C-section instead, which was as easy as booking a hotel room. We would simply arrive one morning, and like magic, leave the next day with a baby. Except this time, Wife was the one who almost died.

Operating tables have large canisters hanging over the side that hold the blood released during an operation. I watched as Wife's canister filled up, and had to be swapped out. Then the new one filled up, too. Her blood pressure plummeted and she began feeling sick. They rushed to get the baby girl out, and she was screaming healthy cries, but things were not going according to schedule. Mom had lost consciousness. The anesthesiologist leapt into action, nervously tweaking dials and scrambling around the table while the surgeon began sowing and tying and clamping like mad. Was this to be a trade of one life for another?

They finally managed to stabilize A.M., but it was too late for me. I had been destabilized by Strike Two, which, once again, I failed to recognize at the time. My illusion of what constitutes a full life for an American man in the 21st century would not die easily. The next morning, our doctor let slip that his current workload included one case in which the baby would die, and another in which the mother would die. And that was just what he was dealing with on that particular day. If I had experienced either of those events, there would have been no need for a Strike Three to jar me out of a lifetime of programming regarding gender roles, economic imperatives, and the existence of elves.

Someone once said that having one kid is like having one kid, but having two is like having ten. That line sounded like just another excuse used by weak parents who cannot control their kids, until the day came for me to bring Wife and Girl home from the hospital. Boy had been at the center of all our attention for his two years on Earth, and he didn't consider sharing the spotlight to be an entirely good thing. "Will we kill her?" he asked. When the answer came back in the negative, he figured he'd try germ warfare instead of sacrificial bloodshed. I had labored to make the house as clean and sanitary as possible for the post-operative ladies, but when the moment came to pick them up, I found Boy sitting in the living room surrounded by a huge puddle of pee and poop that was dripping down the stairs into th edining room and kitchen. That trite old saying about having two kids had proven true before I even had two of them in the house.

Worrying about a wife who had just been sliced open, caring for a hyper-athletic two year old, and changing the 20 diapers that a newborn goes through every 24-hours might have been a busy time, but hey, it would all settle down and I'd go back to chasing the brass ring soon enough. I brought Girl right up to the six-month point without thinking otherwise. Our routine visit to the pediatrician's office seemed like just another step toward that inevitability.

We went to the office in the morning, but left from a hospital that night. A battery of exams and ultrasound images confirmed that both of Girl's thighs were out of their hip joints. She had hip dysplasia, which meant that her pelvis wasn't properly developing the sockets needed to keep her thigh bones in place. It's a common condition that often goes undiagnosed, resulting in varying degrees of disability. The first orthopedic surgeon we saw said that surgery and a hip cast were the only option, followed by reconstructive surgery during adolescence.

Strike Three came through loud and clear. Nothing I was doing at the United Nations or elsewhere was nearly as important as helping this tiny girl to walk. I fired myself from the fast track.

We got a second opinion from surgeon who wanted to try a harness instead of surgery. They put Girl into a tangle of straps and pads that made her look like a tiny paratrooper. She cried for the entire first night, unable to sleep with her legs suspended up and her knees splayed apart so that her thighbones pressed down against her pelvis. I took her to doctor visits nearly every day, during which he made minute adjustments to the harness. As time went by, the visits spread out to three times a week, then to once a week, and finally to twice a month until she was two years old. Every diaper change along the way meant taking off the brace and putting it back on. Meanwhile, her brother was fast showing the size, mobility, and restless energy of the star athlete he would become. Just staying on top of their most basic needs was, surprise, a full-time job.

My wife and I come from vastly different families. I was one of eight kids, and she was one of one. Children in big families typically share the domestic workload, and I was forced to become efficient at the household chores that my wife was able to escape. This imbalance became evident as my scope of work turned out to be larger than your typical husband's, as in doing 100% of everything larger. This was not an easy fate to accept, requiring a degree of self-abnegation uncommon in the modern world, but more on that later.

One day, Girl stood up in her brace and began to walk. Two and a half years later, the doctor said that she could leave it in the office and walk out. Her hip joints were perfect. Mission accomplished. But I was no longer the person who had begun that mission years earlier.

In the paradoxical realm of childcare, three strikes had led me home. Back in the world, people still raced around and piled up money until there was way too much of it and the bucket had to get tipped, and it got tipped the way it always does, not to help the poor, but by warfare, which remains the most efficient way of burning money yet discovered. I opted out of the relentless machinery of hoarding and torching money in favor of the relentless machinery feeding and cleaning up after little people. These are different dimensions entirely, and I feel compelled to report on the universe that I now inhabit in case I am drawn back into that other one, and forget all about the existence of the world that is out of sight and out of mind of those who believe that they run things.

Robinson Crusoe on Venus

I looked now upon the world as a thing remote, which I had nothing indeed to do with, no expectation from, no desires about, nor was likely ever to have: in a word, I thought it look'd as we may perhaps look upon it hereafter.

Daniel DeFoe

I have become a castaway, shipwrecked on the shores of childhood. What's more, I'm not stranded on Mars, a male planet where I might have felt at home, but on Venus, a planet designed and ruled by women. It is indeed an alien environment, though at times I sense that I am the one who's the alien. There are fine young cannibals here who might overrun and eat me alive at any moment. They go for first for the brain, as it is considered a delicacy among them. Much of my gray matter has already been consumed by their near-continuous assaults. I must employ all of my resourcefulness to find my bearings, or I will surely perish in this peculiar world where illogic reigns supreme.

The tools left to me are crude, strange, and come with no directions. There are Diaper Genies who do not grant wishes, other than the partial containment of noxious odors. There are baby slings that do not catapult infants unless used improperly. There are very small jails cunningly called playpens to distract and confuse their prisoners. There are rolling chairs called strollers for tiny people who cannot in fact stroll at all. Even those trustworthy keepers of time, the hours of night and day, no longer follow the same rhythms. Either one can arrive or flee when I'm least expecting it due to the unsteady whims of the little creatures with whom I share this landscape. I must improvise to stay alive.

I traveled widely prior to my crash landing on Venus, and came to be quite comfortable even in the most exotic surroundings. Even so, I now feel lost and adrift, surrounded as I am by beings who value nonsense above all and who are constitutionally incapable of listening to reason. They crawl under carpets instead of walking on them, spit drinks out instead of swallowing them, and hold up yellow snow with bare hands for me to admire. They kick each other in the head, gouge each other's eyes, and hurt themselves in the most perverse ways imaginable, all in the name of intrepid experimentation and brash showmanship.

As I wrote that line, Boy flipped the heavy book he was reading high into the air for no reason at all. It landed squarely on the dog's head, who had been sitting quietly for a change, but who then charged into the table and knocked all the drinks over, which combined into a gray mixture that is now spreading out over the floor. Being immersed in such insanity has prevented me from getting any compass bearing, or to even find the damned compass, which suspiciously disappeared soon after the first one learned to walk. I have been reduced to the desperate measure of writing this letter in a bottle and tossing it into the receding tide. Although I hesitate to provide words of guidance to anyone who might find it, my remaining humanitarian impulses compel me to share the scanty lessons I've learned in any way possible.

First, and perhaps most importantly, I was forced to make peace with my anima—the shadow side of ourselves that so often confounds American males. That way, I was able to begin to understand the strange world that females have created, with its houses and diaper rash creams and K-Marts and sippy cups. We shrink in fear from our female side, for we believe it represents our capacity for being dominated, for losing our freedom, for being beat-up, and sucking at sports. Yet the wise people of the

East, such as Pokeman, Pikachu, and Hello Kitty, teach us that the strong branch breaks under the weight of snow, while the weak one bends and survives. And so, it is okay to wallow for awhile in the wreckage, for ultimately, it is all wreckage to be recycled: this book, this life, this planet. And yet, there is always the strange sensation that, according to Nick Lowe, "I'm crawling, crawling, crawling from the wreckage, into a brand new car."

I therefore endeavor to see myself not as a castaway, but as a person given a second chance to reexamine the world through the eyes of the savage little waifs who accompany me. Their fresh perspective might reveal some hither-too unknown qualities that can help restore my sense of balance and direction. Perhaps a quick look at the expectations embedded in the old world order might be instructive in facing this strange, new one, or at least, prepare me for reentry to it should the opportunity arise.

Koyaanisqatsi

The Hopi have lived in cliff-top villages on mesas high above the Arizona desert for thousands of years. I visited their tribe while researching the topic of First Amendment protection for places that are sacred to practitioners of traditional Native lifeways. The Hopi have tenaciously held onto their traditional beliefs and practices in the face of every effort by the modern world to wipe them out. A central theme in their belief system is the concept of balance: balance with nature, with each other, and with the great mystery. This is no surprise since survival on those sun-blasted mesas depends upon remaining in balance with the water cycle. Balance is so important to the Hopis that they have a single word to describe life out of balance: Koyaanisqatsi. It is also, of course, the title of an enigmatic film by Godfrey Reggio that portrays the impact of technology on modern life. After I first took up the work of raising children, it seemed to me that I had upset the balance of nature and was in a state of

36

Koyaanisqatsi. Life had become precarious because old systems had been overturned but new ones had yet to emerge. This was around 2005, and there were very few other SAHDs out there. Now, there are more than 3 million of us, but certain aspects of the challenge of finding a new balance remains unchanged.

All you have to do is look at the variety of tasks that must get done in a family, and who is supposed to do them, according to the inertia rolling your way from the past couple thousand years. Some people like to use the word "roles" to describe the division of labor, but as someone who manages projects, I much prefer to think in terms of scopes of work. The concept of roles is way too vague, and it sets up artificial boundaries and taboos, both of which were probably designed to ensure the extraction of a reliable profit stream from the family unit in a centralized economy. The scope of work was divvyed-up pretty clearly between the husband and the wife: the husband sold his time while the woman nurtured the next generation. He got the mortgage while she made the house into a home. He dealt with the plumbing while she changed the diapers. She did the shopping and cooked the dinner while he did the dishes. The man shoveled the snow and the woman handled the laundry. He mowed the lawn, she planted the garden, and so on. Now, let's say that your wife goes to work for someone besides her family. She will have neither the time nor the energy to perform the tasks assigned to her by tradition. If you're a SAHD, and you do everything that you were supposed to do except sell your time, plus everything that she was supposed to do, then you will truly be done. The stress will build to stroke-inducing levels, and her requests to do even the most menial favor will be met with a vituperative reply that goes far beyond, "do it yourself." You will become a nasty, haggard, unshaven brute. Life will be out of balance and you will be headed straight toward the nearest mesa cliff. Luckily, before that happened to me, I was struck by an insight in the form of an Etch-A-Sketch.

One day while caring for my hyperactive toddler and hyperathletic 5 year-old, plus simultaneously performing the entire scope of work listed above for all parties, except carrying the majority cash burden, I found myself exhausted to the point where standing up was not an option. I lay down on the couch for a moment of rest, but the minute I closed my eyes, WHAMO! The corner of an Etch-A-Sketch crashed down against my temple. Until that epiphany, I never realized that those hefty, solid red plastic toys are built to withstand space travel, or that even a two-year old girl had the power to knock me out. For a brief shining moment, amidst the galaxies and stars of the universe, I became one with that unnamable, dynamic equilibrium to which we all aspire. Koyaanisqatsi became a thing of the past. Then I came to, and an unquenchable desire rose up within me to finally see the magic behind the screen of an Etch-A-Sketch. I bashed it open on the stone path leading to our front door, and found that it is indeed a marvel of engineering and slight-of-hand. But my anger was misplaced, because Etch-A-Sketches don't kill people. Toddlers armed with Etch-A-Sketches kill people. I had heard that naps have been shown to enhance a person's functioning and even extends their lives, but in my house, they are life-threatening events. Another time, I awoke from one to find Boy firing a high-powered staple gun point blank at my face, just for fun.

These near-death experiences made me realize, however, that life has an indescribable poignancy, dare I say, a sacredness, that is beyond the understanding of our rational consciousness. It also made me realize that there is not enough time in the day to untangle the paradox of chasing balance. Just say no to the nonessentials, and put off everything else until they go to college.

Why Not Stay At Home?

In a word: testicles. Many thousands of years ago, a proto-human father decided to flee the household cave after having his gonads repeatedly struck by children. The fact that these strikes were accidental mattered little to him—he was out of there, either permanently, or until those little buggers were safely asleep. Hence began the unfortunate trend of fathers abandoning their families, or at least spending long hours commuting. The Bible tries to cover up this reality by claiming that Adam put on a loincloth because he was ashamed. The real reason was that he was just trying to protect his specials from the constant battering dealt out by the wee little people, who spend years within just the right height range to inflict painful collateral damage from their twirling, staggering, and stumbling about. It's ironic that kids should inflict so many insults on the very things that helped give them life in the first place. Perhaps they find the family jewels to be appropriate targets for expressing their rage at being stuck in a mysterious place ruled by giants who seem bent on bossing them around and enforcing capricious rules.

So before accepting the mission I'm outlining here, you must ask yourself, do I feel lucky enough to avoid getting my nuts elbowed, punched, head-butted, and mashed with shoulders on a daily basis? Well, do you, punk?

Wait a minute now. My business sense is tingling. I'll turn the painful side of being a SAHD into a moneymaking windfall by inventing the Kid Kup! YES! This specially designed athletic cup will care for the caretaker by protecting you from the incidental abuse inflicted by your oblivious little ones. Are you tired of reading in bed to a toddler when they raise up a leg, and without a care in the world, let it fall straight down between your's? Or how about when they trip, and as they're falling down, grab hold of that safety handle protruding so conveniently from your lower abdomen? Have you lost all inhibition to reflexively protecting your crotch while standing next to your child in playgrounds, grocery stores, and other public places? Such socially unacceptable and otherwise embarrassing behavior can now be eliminated thanks to the Kid Kup! Mothers would once again allow their children to have playdates with yours without worrying that perhaps you're warped in that particular way. No, there would be no more worries. So look for the Kid

Kup wherever diapers are sold, and never get out of bed without it.

Even now, as if on cue while I sit writing these words, I received a painful bite on the thigh. Girl might be only two years old, but she knows how to get my utmost attention. Did I smack her away? No. I did not. What I did instead was to stop writing this book for a number of years until her height and available brain power eliminated my need for a Kid Kup. Something had to give, and it turned out to be my scribbling in favor of food service, chauffeuring, house cleaning, and manually protecting my crotch area. I suppose it is all for the best since the job of getting the Kid Kup into stores would have opened up opportunities for my kids to invent other painful reminders that I'm not paying enough attention to them. Alas, once again the entrepreneurial spirit has escaped me.

Yet I must confess to not being entirely scribbling-free. During the fleeting 3 hours of daycare time, I continue to attempt to make sense of the grand movements of the United Nations in dealing with the ongoing destruction of our home planet by a certain singular species. In that endeavor, I feel as though I've won a thousand battles, yet we are all losing the war. At least they pay me a day rate that contributes to our ability to do whatever it is that we do around here.

Another chilling fact emerging from this miasma is that men are probably not meant to raise children. We're meant to slay mammoths, mate, and die fighting off attackers, hopefully in that order. But for me it is too late to die young. Instead, I'm on the inside of a world reserved for women since the dawn of time, and let me tell you, I don't belong here. And yet, I recommend that more fathers take on the job of being their children's primary caretaker. This ironic situation can only be reconciled by the fact that I have emerged from the cauldron of childcare as kind of a crazy Zen fool. Relinquishing one's old identity, or in my case, having it stolen from you and melted down, can be enormously freeing, unless of course you're an infallible master of the universe, in which case there is no hope for you or others in your orbit.

Rude Baptisms on a Blue Planet

In case you were wondering, the answer is yes--I'm full of shit. It's on my clothes, hands, face, and even in my dreams. If you've been initiated into the Mystical Order of Ass Wipers, then you, too, are full of shit, and the bond between reader and writer has never been stronger. If you have not been initiated, or as Jimmy Hendrix would say, *experienced*, you might want to skip this chapter. Hendrix could sense that a profound state of being was out there somewhere, waiting for him, but he died before he actually got the chance to become experienced, because only kids can *experience* you. Nothing else really works. Not drugs, not alcohol, not groupies, not "god." So fire your nanny and follow me to the yellow waters and night soil that await you in the promised land.

Men or women who claim to be raising kids while also enjoying worldly achievement will never be experienced because they're either outsourcing their child raising, or they have a spouse who's doing the work and protecting them from being experienced. Alexander the Great couldn't have conquered his own hometown if he'd been taking care of kids. Hitler would have stayed a failed painter if only one or two little souls had found their cosmic way into his life. Had these and countless other psychopaths been taking care of kids, the world would have been a better place by their absence from it. I am not sure what that says about me.

At any rate, the precise moment when you've been experienced on this job will register somewhere deep in your soul, and if you're the genuine article, experienced you shall be. My own personal baptism arrived unbidden after I tried following the advice of a scatological liar who had written a popular childcare book. He said that the main trick to potty training was to not backtrack under any circumstances--once the diapers come off, keep them off. In practical terms, this means that they will go in their pants, or snowsuit, or ballerina outfits until they decide that you've had enough. It could take weeks or months before they choose to worship the porcelain god before all others, but in the meantime, they'll be crapping their pants and getting it all over you day and night. The distinctly religious aspect of this work become apparent when you reach your poop handling limit, and you either snap, or you enter an altered state that opens up a whole different horizon.

In my case, I was stewing in a mess of toddler manure from October to May of the following year. Winter clothes added a dose of the macabre to the situation, which might have accelerated my breaking on through to the other side. Upon returning from even a short trip to the store, I'd have to change soaked underwear, pants and plastic pants, plus wiping the butt that remained a bit soiled from our emergency outdoor underwear change that occurred during our outing. She would soak her pants 5 times a day, plus wake me every morning at 4am in desperate need of freshening up. Just when I'd think she was potty-trained, she'd have a soggy breakdown on the sidewalk and revert to her old ways as if no progress had ever been made. Against the backdrop of the potty training blues, the clarion call to "help wipe me!" would ring out several times a day from Boy, which is better than if he did not wipe at all and let his underwear do the job.

Boy liked to break with tradition by sitting directly on the toilet's porcelain instead of lowering the seat. He would in variably slip off, with pee and poop flying everywhere. Instead of changing one diaper, I'd have to clean the whole bathroom. This went on for quite some time before the dog decided to join the party, and began pooping in the dining room. I admit that I was a tough case: it took three incontinent animals living, breathing, and excreting in my house in order to properly baptize me into the Mystical Order. But it was upon my initiation that I realized I would need to write this book if I were to survive the long twilight struggle in which I am now engaged.

While we're on the topic of elimination, I would like to bequeath unto you a childcare technique that's a veritable golden nugget you won't find in any other book. If you have a girl, you must learn to hold her up by her thighs, with her back propped up against your chest, so she can pee or even poop outdoors without splattering either of you. This is an amazing move that I've used countless times in a variety of settings to save everyone's day. Your learning it here is worth one hundred times the price of this book.

So onward we journeyed, steadfast before the porcelain god, coaxing Girl to join in the worship that we all enjoy. Amidst the chaos of failing to potty-train her and constantly wiping Boy, a break though in my worldview opened before: we are all maintenance men, and the sooner we realize our essential role, the better chance we'll have of keeping the planet habitable. This applics to everyone, but apparently, we'd rather go extinct as a species than admit it and act accordingly.

One day, Boy announced, "I hypnotized Girl to go to the potty!" I laughed it off, but then realized that she did indeed use the potty consistently that day. I had a five year-old hypnotist! Why didn't I think of that? Perhaps someone has to rise above the level of maintenance man. Her grand moment of gaining full control over her bowels was duly celebrated. Sometimes it takes a Holy Fool to show you what a bloody impatient fool you can be.

So let us close by raising our voices in praise of excrement, which symbolizes a holism, a symmetry, if you will. My daughter might be cleaning me up one day, as I had to recently clean up one of my parents' messes in the wake of surgery and intestinal viruses. Engage in this cycle and you will be experienced, you will be baptized, and you will be in harmony with the universe.

Our First Son Wore a Dog Suit

An old friend taught me everything I needed to know about child-raising. He stressed the need for regular mealtimes, daily exercise, and consistent discipline. Most of all, he taught me how to earn love and respect by being what I'll call an alpha friend. That's the kind of person who makes decisions by taking everyone's wishes into consideration, while also accepting responsibility for their safety and wellbeing. If you can do that, it's more likely they will follow you peaceably, and if they don't follow you, you're perfectly justified in carrying them along kicking and screaming.

My old friend survived alligator attacks, hurricanes, tornadoes, blizzards, rip-tides, lyme disease, and just about every other rock that mother nature can throw at you. He also found a way to get into trouble every single day of his very long and happy life. In other words, dealing with Duke the wonder dog was perfect practice for raising kids.

It's a short trip from being a dog whisperer to being a baby wrestler and alpha friend. Hence I will spare you the need to digest all of the parenting books that clutter Amazon's endless shelves. The only tricks you'll need to know are contained in this one short chapter.

At first, I didn't want the responsibility of a dog. I finally felt it was time for children. Wife didn't want children yet, but she wanted a dog. We compromised and got both. The other conflict to resolve concerned the fact that I was raised with the understanding that I was to do what my parents asked me to do, when they asked me to do it, and with no return commentary on my part. There was no other way to wrangle eight kids running in different directions all the time. On the other hand, Wife was raised with the grace of knowing that her opinion was worthy of consideration, even if that opinion sometimes involved a reversal of the parent/child decision making process. Our differing views about whether to have children, and how to deal with children if confronted with them, would be resolved thanks to the blond wolf-dog puppy we adopted and named Duke, after Duke Kahanamoku, the legendary waterman of Hawaii. Duke became the subject of an experiment designed to educate a child-free couple about how to keep another animal alive and behaving with a modicum of civility in their house. Because he could not entirely grasp the implications of his predicament, he stepped gladly into the role of understudy for our #1 Son.

At first, we tried training him on our own, but he was wild and tough and we learned something new: mixed breeds that include strong Chow strains will do strangely aggressive things, such as developing signature Judo moves to be performed on unsuspecting deliverymen. Duke's throw was spectacularly effective, yet involved no teeth on skin. He would grab a pant leg and get all four paws pulling full speed in reverse until the man went down. I would run to the rescue, only to find Duke looking up at me gleefully as if to say, "hey! Look what I found in the yard!" But I was an ungrateful owner who did not want deliverymen delivered to my front door. This sport became so much fun for him that it soon became necessary to call in professional help.

Our dog trainer was a retired Miami K-9 police officer who immediately identified the problem: in Duke's opinion, we were all just buddies. Wife and I had diverging approaches to training, and so Duke concluded that he could divide and conquer us, leaving the pack hierarchy basically flat. He then felt perfectly justified to do what he pleased most of the time. The trainer said we would have to jointly express our dominance over him, and keep expressing it in a unified voice, until he realized that although we were all spirits sharing a journey through the material world, he was under our authority while he remained under our roof. We had to firmly and consistently reinforce behaviors that we expected. He might eventually get a glimmer of understanding that these actions were for his own happiness, and the happiness of those around him.

Authors of how-to-raise-your-child books like to make it complicated, but it's really simple. You must be a benevolent dictator who lives for the singular purpose of serving the masses. If a child decides to turn on you with bad behavior, or on themselves with self-destructive behavior, the root of the problem is the same: you are not serving their personal growth toward responsibility for their own freedom.

Now, problems seem to arise because some parents don't know how they want their kids to act anymore. For example, schools are bombarding students with anti-bullying programs in an attempt to balance out bad parenting. These programs are entirely ineffectual because when the bully is identified, it certainly cannot be my wonderful and perfect son or daughter. The hierarchy quickly gets flattened back out, and the issue slides until somebody shows up at school with a gun. The trick is to try to understand the experiences that your child is going through, listen carefully to their problems, do your best to offer wise counsel, and never stop issuing the orders. You're the leader of the pack, the circus ringmaster who keeps the tigers in their place and the clowns having fun. Show them how to limit their own worst impulses by getting your smart phone addiction under control, and how to become the unique creation that they are by finding ways to express your own, even if they go completely against the grain of our post-industrial zombie consumer mindset.

One thing I do not want to do here, though, is to glaze over the challenges of keeping a dog when you also have kids. Puppies drink deeply from your well of patience, leaving precious little for your children, who will pay the price when it runs dry and your temper flares from the well fracked by too many distractions. Grown-up dogs aren't much easier, and they'll raise the roof with thunderous barking just when you thought that a moment of peace might be descending upon you, your house and your life.

Duke is almost as needy and expensive as my human children, so I figure that he counts as half a child, which brings us up to the requisite US average of 2.5 kids. But he is toying with that statistic because he is really too smart to be a dog, and he knows it. If I ask him to fetch a ball, he'll go get it, but if I throw it again, he'll look up at me with pity for displaying such stupidity, as if to say, "I just went and got that ball for you. If you persist in throwing it, you'll have to go fetch it yourself."

On the upside, a dog will get your fat ass out of the house for a walk after dinner. Don't underestimate the value of this moment away from the tumult--the life you save could be your own. If you take your young kids along on the dog walk, remember to bring two bags, because when the dog goes, your kid will take it as a cue and insist that they, too, must perform a #2 on the spot. The first time this happened, one kid heaved a dump right next to Duke's on the grass strip that runs next to the sidewalk. There was simply no choice. It was either there or in the pants. It lies there still. But I shall retrieve it shortly, and forever after carry at least two bags on my nightly excursions.

Duke the golden wolf-dog lived to be 17 years old. Two months before he exited this corporeal existence, a six week-old Chow-lab puppy appeared at the local animal shelter. The symmetry was undeniable. Whereas Duke was yellow with eyes that glowed like amber lights in the dark, this one is a black fluff ball with retinas that burn a piercing green fire. We took him home to meet the dog who taught both of our kids to walk by grabbing onto his thick fur; the dog who cycled between both their bedsides every night on self-imposed sentry duty, the dog who understood everything we said, and who showed us that we could raise children together, after all. The bear-like little pup saw that he had huge paws to fill, and so he turned and commenced chewing up the scenery, just like his older cousin had so many years earlier.

Ode to Needy Angels

Here's another thing that the childcare books won't tell you: raising kids will put you in touch with your inner divinity. The little people around here will get down on their knees and pray to me with tears rolling down their faces as if the world were coming to an end, all for a squeezy yogurt. When they turn on the fire hose of begging and pleading, I gain some inkling into how God must feel to be on the receiving end of humanity's unceasing prayers. Just like us grown-ups, the list of things they want is endless. God also knows that if I'm ever foolish enough to try to satisfy them, the list will reset back to the beginning, and the beseeching will start all over again. So I try to not go down that road. I take the path less traveled by, which I have learned from my inner toddler and Nancy Reagan, who must have something in common: I just say NO. Or when I'm feeling soft, YES, but not now, which inevitably triggers the rapid response, "when?" To which I respond, "when you've been good," which jump starts negotiations and I regret ever forsaking the wisdom of NO. Perhaps these vacillations reflect my search for a way to reconcile Samuel Beckett and James Joyce. Beckett said that the answer is always the same--NO. But Joyce ended it all with a seemingly eternal YES. The truth is, they're both right, and being a baby wrestler means having a firm command of each.

The begging and pleading you will face comes from the fact that kids are a salesman's dream. First off, they'll believe literally anything; the more fanciful, the better. Next, they have no conception of the value of money. In their eyes, a shiny copper penny is more impressive and exciting than a dull green slip of paper with Benjamin Franklin's picture on it. What more could a salesman ask for in a sucker? That one is born every minute? How about eight born every minute in the US alone? The icing on the cake is that whatever you sell to them will be quickly out-grown, and they'll be back shortly in dire need of more. Kids are the American Dream consumer, with no end to their burning desires for all the stuff they see on dancing across screens large and small, that perfect sales agent for consumer fun-land. As a result, I see homes overflowing with plastic in a perverse variety of shapes and vivid primary colors that scream out at you in a kind of reverse camouflage. Suburbia has replaced farms that grow food with farms that grow plastic. It grows out of the lawn and up from living room floors. Most of it cannot even be recycled, so into the landfill it shall go where it will remain for millions of years.

Take "Power Rangers" for example, which made some entrepreneur into a multi-billionaire despite the idiotic conceits that pass for stories on the TV series, which are in themselves commercials intended to sell the plastic people. Or how about transformers—machines that turn into other machines, which is a brilliant conceit that programs young minds for a future of endlessly upgrading their high-tech devices? These toys are rapidly transformed into dust-gathering detritus strewn behind the couch. In our case, all of our plastic was scavenged from roadsides or garage sales. I assuage my eco-conscience thusly. Plastic, it seems we must have you, but you are the Great Satan, and the Screen is your handmaiden.

Standing amidst this debris scattered across our great nation, I see children bored with it all, waiting for someone to play with them. Even an adult would suffice, such as the kids' parents, but it was they who bought all that stuff in the first place hoping that they were buying some time for themselves while the plastic occupies the kid. Their hopes were dashed when the kid played with the item for 15 hot minutes, and then spent another 5 trying to break the insulting object. Regardless of price, such toys bring a standard total of 20 minutes of free time before becoming non-biodegradable clutter.

I was heading down this infernal route when I saw that I am not only a fool, but that as such, I am also the greatest toy that any toddler could dream up. They understood this fact before I did, which is why they will not let me sit reading or writing, which is idle in their view, when I could be of full service to them in the fun business. So don't let your kids become plastic addicts, pleading for one toy or electronic devices after another, while you become the desperate enabler, ever more anxious to shut them up with poor substitutes for the attention--the zany, irrational, irreverent, comic attention that they crave and that only you can provide.

Wait a minute! Hold the presses! I just read in the New York Times that the advertising technique of product placement has now infiltrated the book publishing business. Little commercials for this or that consumer item will begin popping up in novels, just like they already do in movies. Hello Madison Avenue! As I already pointed out, kids are a marketing goldmine, so just let me know what product you'd like to sell, and I'll insinuate it right into this book. How about the latest candy that's guaranteed to attack kids' enamel with the ferocity of a red ant storm? Better yet, what about a video game with fight scenes so eerily compelling and intoxicating that your kids will look like zombies when watching them? Alas, I may have shot myself in the foot yet again. The big bucks will pass me by on their happy search for greedy grown-ups who're anxious to exploit the little people, and exploited they shall be.

The Milk-Plus Bar

Bring your baby to a bar, preferably a singles bar, so that when they begin to squall, couples will glance over at the source of the noise, see their possible future, and look back with glazed eyes at the person who might one day deliver that noise unto them. It's great fun to watch an infant transform the atmosphere in these places, causing a sudden shift in the laws of attraction, and unmasking true character and intention. Some young couples perk up and talk more animatedly upon see a baby, while others cringe and seem to withdraw from each other. Then there are those who react in opposing ways, with one happy and the other grim, telegraphing doom for that particular relationship. We always felt free to invade these hallowed placcs in lower Manhattan with babies. Perhaps it's unfair to use your infant to create unscripted theatre for your own personal enjoyment, but it was great free entertainment.

Our first foray into a chic bar with baby occurred while attempting to treat cabin fever. We were wandering the winter streets of Soho, which were beautiful in the swirling snow, until his messy diaper signaled the need for professional attention. Changing his diaper was often a rigorous maneuver, but performing it on a stoop in the bitter cold while snow settled onto his bareness strained my technical expertise to the point where an immediate infusion of alcohol became imperative. I tossed him back into the sling and we all repaired to the nearest unfrozen watering hole.

The Cub Room was a semi-high-brow pick-up spot that enjoyed a decent run on Sullivan Street but is now defunct. On that night, we ventured inside warily, half expecting to get turned away like Mary and Joseph in their similar predicament some years earlier, but no one stopped us. Our luck continued when we managed to find two seats at the crowded bar. I held baby with one hand, a beer with the other, and reflected on how the warmth of that place and the coolness of my beer were rewards for my expert handling of his various needs. Then he caught sight of me enjoying a glass of frothy golden liquid, and began demanding one for himself with great urgency. Under normal conditions, I might have felt reticent to let my wife bare her breast in a pheromone-filled barroom, but once again, baby's need overcame any sense of decorum. So we sat at the bar and all enjoyed a good drink.

There is something about a baby breastfeeding at a singles bar that harkens back to a simpler era. Like around twelve hundred years ago. Bartenders probably didn't mind it back then either, and they certainly don't mind it now. They're so bored with all the repetitive adult preening that nothing could be more refreshing than the sight of a tiny man getting a free drink. They know that there should be more babies in these places. Little tikes should be encouraged to come out for happy hours, and get paraded about as living testaments to the end result of the veiled sexual maneuvers unfolding around them. They lay bare the fulfillment of our deepest natural urge for all to see. So go forth, procreate, and bring your baby to the bars. Show the horny people what they're actually aiming for with their high paying jobs and gym memberships. Clue: it's not sex. That's just nature's ruse.

While ensconced at the bar in the Cub Room, I had a moment of awakening that marked my transition to middle age. Normally, a fish cannot see the water in which it swims, but thanks to the undeniable reality of the baby who was staring me in the face contrasted with all the other people who remained in a different universe, I suddenly knew that I was middle aged. Some might argue that maturity came late for me, and I would agree, if childcare had not mysteriously turned back my mental clock. For me, middle age had become much more like childhood than the young-adulthood I had more recently left behind, because I no longer have any trouble making a fool of myself. All you have to do is consider this book for a moment and you'll agree. But then again, if you're doing this work yourself, you already know that inspired foolery might be one's highest achievement on any given day. Today happens to be April 1st, but I'm being totally serious here.

All the other child raising books drum home the idea that during adolescence, boys are more immature than girls. What they don't tell you is that we remain that way forever, thank God. It is the one competitive advantage that men bring to the job of childcare: we might be better able to access the child within us. After a short time on the job, you begin to glimpse the wisdom of being a fool, and the longer you're on the job, the bigger fool you become, in the best possible way. A holy fool doesn't hold onto a shred of the hubris so highly prized by modern society—the type that causes war profiteering, famines, child slavery, murder, robbery, and film production. To do this job well, you must strip off the veneer of adulthood, let go of your self-importance, and rejoin the kids in their games.

Research shows that children who spend lots of time with their fathers benefit from higher grades, greater motivation, fewer anxiety disorders, and a reduced risk of delinquency or teen pregnancy. The flip side is that fathers who take care of children lose IQ points, jettison ambition as it is popularly defined, suffer bouts of anxiety, risk dropping out of the workforce, and might just get the neighbor's Au Pair pregnant. Every fool knows that the universe maintains a fearful symmetry. The trick is to know when you're being a fool, as opposed to just being an idiot.

A Moveable Feast

I was awakened this morning by Boy's announcement that Girl was splashing her feet in the dog's water bowl. Now that I've been experienced, I try not to get uptight about that kind of news. My calm reaction provoked Boy into adding that it was unfair: she was drinking so much of the water that there would soon be none left for Duke. That cued another adrenaline pumping dash down the stairs, this time to stop Girl from imbibing any more germ-ridden, slobbery dog water. There are not enough degrees of separation in the following equation: the dog likes to drink from the toilet, Girl likes to drink from the dog's bowl, and I like to drink Girl's leftover milkshakes. I'll have to cut out the shakes, because they're the only link in the chain over which I have any control.

If you do choose to take on this mission, get ready to be shocked and awed by the non-food items that kids will seek out and eat.

They're not picky eaters when it comes to things that they are not supposed to eat, like crispy lead paint chips, flavorful plastic pens, and chewy rubber bands. They will gnaw the tires off toy cars, apply glue stick to their lips, and look at you with an oddly blank gaze while letting dozens of pennies dribble out of their mouths. You'll often find yourself yelling incongruous commands, like "get that canoe out of your mouth!" Your attempts to stay organized by making lists will be foiled, because lists are one of the tastiest items on a toddler's menu. Mine bolt them down like spies who get caught with the names of people in deep cover. But of all the delicacies to be had, the real prize is gum that has already been chewed by a stranger and spit out onto the sidewalk where it can receive proper seasoning with crunchy bits of concrete, asphalt and various unmentionables. Kids will wait until you're not looking to pry such a glob of old pink gum off the sidewalk, secrete it in their clothes, and then retrieve it later on when the moment seems right to recycle a nice piece of filth-studded bubblegum. Tell-tale smacking sounds will come from the backseat while you're driving the car, or from the high chair while you're fixing dinner, and your adrenal system will get yet another unwelcomed jolt. The contortions you will do when you catch them enjoying one of those horrible globs will only succeeded in driving the behavior further underground.

Just when you thought it couldn't get any worse, you will hear "look Dad!" In my case, Boy was pointing out an intrepid taste tests being performed by his 18 month-old sister. (One can only wonder what I didn't catch him eating since there was no one around to call him out on it). This time, I see Girl holding up 2 fingers that resemble mud popsicles. Before I can stop her, she puts those poop-covered fingers, which had come from a successful exploration of her dirty diaper, directly into her mouth. Then a few days after witnessing this abomination, we were outside when I turned to see Boy cupping a mound of snow in his bare hands that was drenched in dog-pee like a giant lemon snow cone from hell. Yum! What is it with these mad elves?

But perhaps the most hair-raising incident came while I was relaxing for a brief moment in the hammock. Girl offered me a long stemmed shoot of grass, and I let it dangle from my mouth like I was a carefree hayseed from a bygone era. Of course, she put one into her mouth, too, and immediately started choking to death on it. I struggled to remove the stringy obstruction while she was gagging and coughing and panicking and not breathing. After what seemed like an eternity, she finally spit half of it out and swallowed the other half. Boy celebrated by kicking his football through a window. So ended another nice relaxing time in the idyllic backyard hammock.

Then there was the time I heard the unmistakable throaty sound of gagging coming from the other room. I rushed in to find

Girl's windpipe neatly plugged by a marble she had somehow dislodged from a little game. One would think that such a brush with death would change her ways. Hardly. She still chews on rubber bands whenever and wherever she finds them in a habit that would continue for about half a decade.

Dinnertime is also murder, or more accurately, accidental suicide. I waste half of my life cooking for little dinner guests who would much prefer to snack on their toxic made-in-China toys. The meal-time stress that multiple children can place upon you shows first in the intestines, which begin producing hellacious volumes of gas because you must gulp down meals while trying to keep them in their chairs, glasses of milk on the table, and food out of their windpipes, all while jumping up every 15 seconds to deal with the results of one of these inevitabilities. As a result, your poor intestines bloat like balloon art. From there, the tension creeps into your organs and slowly squeezes the life out of them. It feels fatal and doesn't put one in the mood to bath two screaming kids.

In the days before Heimlich invented his maneuver, one had to rely upon the "blessing of throats." This was a semi-sacrament during which a priest would cross two large candles, scissor-like over your throat, and say a special choke-prevention prayer. Even at 8 years old, I knew it was superstition, but it was a pretty ominous warning to do everything I could to work with, instead

69

of against, the basic laws of physics. Mothers were the principal beneficiaries of this prayer, because the task of insinuating food, but nothing else, safely into children's stomachs is the main reason why mothers are so exhausted at the end of every day. In addition to watching everything that goes into a child's mouth, these poor women are solely and entirely responsible for every other event thoughout the day and the night that endangers their kids' lives. And they are legion. The adrenaline flows in bursts throughout the day as kids heedlessly engage in life-threatening activities, and by bedtime you're totally shot. It's one thing for a child to die while in the care of its mother, the person who gave it life, who is closer to it than anyone in the world. If a man came home to such bad news, he'd probably be most concerned with comforting his wife, but if a woman came home to such news, there would probably be another death—his. That's another reason why the roles have been divided up amongst the sexes in the way they are now. Men simply refused to accept such existential responsibility. It's more than most of us can handle.

In Praise of Fair to Middling Babysitters

Babysitters are like drugs and alcohol. They're expensive, addictive, and escapist. But I love my children so very much when someone else is taking care of them. They become the very finest children I can imagine after a babysitter has been in charge of the real things for only two hours. Halos illuminate their precious little heads, and nostalgia sweeps away all the anguish they cause me. Babysitters are drugs that can make your world appear to be a better place, but use them wisely. Beware of falling into the common trap of fooling yourself into thinking that you have the drug under control, and that you are raising your own children, when in fact you are outsourcing the job. This is a manifestation of the managerial culture taking over our consciousness. The reality is that you are not raising your kids if someone else is covering more than a few hours a week of your childcare time. You are then managing the person who is raising your kids. These are not the same things. I have done it both ways, and I am proud to say that I have weaned myself off that particular drug. Yet I take my sobriety one day at a time, ever vigilant against the temptation to believe that more babysitting time will make all of my problems disappear.

If you want to grasp the indescribable experience that I am trying to describe in this book, you'll have to cut your sitter time down to no more than five hours per week. That'll give you enough time with the little critters to know what I'm talking about. Should you find yourself overindulging, you can reduce your babysitting time and the accompanying withdrawal symptoms by exploiting the natural lifecycle that occurs with all babysitters, nannies, au pairs, or whatever your particular drug of choice may be. Your typical sitter never lasts more than 12 months: 6 months to burn out, 4 more months to come to truly loath your kids, and then six weeks to find what they think will be a better position. The cycle will then begin all over again. This will happen no matter how nice your kids or how patient the sitter. There is simply an outer limit to the amount of time any human can do this job if the little torturers are not your own. So when their 12 months are up, let the sitter go, join our ranks, and consider yourself in recovery. You might have relapses, but that's okay. The Betty Ford Clinic wasn't built in a day.

Beyond the obvious downsides of outsourcing the development of your child's character, there lurks another hazard to sitter overuse that I must discuss with you now. When hiring babysitters, you will be tempted to take on the most attractive woman available, preferably one who is a total knockout. She might not possess the skills you need, but she has the look you want. Remember that Elke Sommer was an au pair. Each year, a large number of American men turn their addiction into a fulltime lifestyle by running off with their nubile young babysitters. SAHDs who work at home may be most at risk. Think about it. What happens when you wake up one morning to find a beautiful woman in your house who's underfoot all day while your kids are at school, and then all night when your wife is away on business trips? So get that monkey off your back, no matter how pretty she might be.

Here In Zombie Land

Despite the drawbacks, you will find that television is the quickest and cheapest way to get kids out of your hair. Instant relief will be delivered unto you by letting them bask in the green slime that spreads out across the living room floor, or in the insidious glow from mini-screens wherever they may be. Who cares if the hand that rocks the cradle, and therefore rocks the world, belongs to corporate giants bent on creating an uncontrollable addiction in your child? Pop media deals out the opium of the masses, especially for kids, to which some parents say, thank you, Lord! As long as they can put their little marauding hecklers in front of that screen and not hear a peep out of them for hours, let them become zombies. Zombies are easier to control. Who cares if the kiddie dope pouring from the squalid wasteland of corporate media will prevent them from being able to concentrate for more than the few seconds? The new national scourge that we call attention deficit disorder certainly has nothing to do with those quickly dancing images that require so little intellectual engagement. The screens are getting smarter and the people are getting dumber, but no one seems to care. Here in Zombieland, everyone is programmed to stare at their screens for as much of their lives as possible. Do not ask any troubling questions. Except perhaps one: who lives in a pineapple under the sea? If you don't know the answer to this question, you either do not have kids, or you live in Krygistan.

In restaurants one now commonly sees families in which everyone is staring down at their own mini-screens with nary a word passing between them for the entire meal. The kids hold the screens surreptitiously under the table, just like they see their parents doing, so they can stare downward rather than confront the awful reality of reality. Sometimes only the kids are on the screens, but even then, the parents aren't talking. They're too dazed and confused by their own over-use of the screen during the workday to carry on a conversation. It turns out that American Indians were right: pictures, and especially moving pictures, can steal your soul. The twist is that the soul captured belongs to the viewer, not to the subject. Almost all programming, whether delivered via TV or the internet, exists to numb our minds into the torpor necessary to make us vulnerable to sales pitch. The new rallying cry should be, "Zombies of the world, unite! You have nothing to lose but your souls!"

"Dad, did you know that Santa Claus is the patron saint of hookers?" Boy asked. I admitted that I was ill-informed about that particular mystical connection, and inquired where he had learned of it. "I dunno. Maybe on the show about a two-headed pig and a Cyclops that lived for one hour." That was a perfect illustration of the educational aspects of TV. I asked him whether he thought TV was a good thing, but he stumped me once again by saying, "without TV, all those people wouldn't be able to show their creativity," meaning those who serve up the onscreen pablum. I found it hard to argue with that sad fact. For at this very minute, there are thousands of smart people: writers and actors trained at NYU, programmers with degrees from MIT, marketers from Harvard, and rapacious lawyers from Yale all slaving away to bring you reality shows like "Pregnant and Dating" or video games like "Muslim Massacre: the Game of Religious Genocide." Banks of brilliant minds on both coasts labor day and night to steal the eyes of 8 year-olds whose parents just want them to sit down and shut up. But Boy was correct. The time spent by all those bright young professionals who make "content" is keeping them out of trouble. As long as they keep producing that trash and selling the airtime that keeps it afloat, then maybe, just maybe, they won't use their time and talents to dream up mutant financial instruments, build better bombs, or design more efficient ways to rape the Earth. TV is therefore our kid's way of saving the world from the potential evil wrought by adults.

Some parents believe that we can control screen access to make sure that the "good" comes through while the "bad" gets blocked. Keep fooling yourselves. Kids will always reach the forbidden fruit. At six years old, Boy found a fine use for the TiVo: replaying a commercial for "Girls Gone Wild" over and over. I came into the room one morning and found that technological marvel (which is already long outdated as I edit this entry) obeying his every command. "Hey Dad, look at this!" he said excitedly, "I think this video is for boys. Can you get me Girls Gone Wild? There are *three volumes!*" Another time, I gave 5 year-old Girl the remote control because I needed her out of the way for a moment. I'd forgotten that we'd recently changed telecom providers, and I hadn't yet explored all the places that the new provider was happy to take their customers, which is always the same--straight to hell, as long as you pay your monthly fee. I walked past the living room and glanced at the TV, expecting to see Dora and Boots. Instead, the screen was filled with sweaty, topless women romping around a weight lifting room. She was watching a cinematic masterpiece called "Sex Pot" which ingeniously combines sex and drugs by telling the story of two marijuana dealers and their fatuous female accomplices. Girl didn't complain at all when I shut that thing down because she had already deemed the show's story line and production values to be seriously subpar.

While on vacation in Vermont one summer, I accidentally discovered the antidote to the kiddie dope of screen gazing. Boy was six, and his enormous energy, always percolating at high boil, turned toward badgering me to watch TV. At that moment, I wanted to read and was tempted to just say yes. Instead, I took him out to explore the stream that was hidden behind a bank of trees in back of the condo. It turned out to be a sparkling clear cascade flowing over a bed of smooth, multicolored stones and boulders. The water seemed freezing cold at first, but we soon got used to it, and began walking upstream until we reached a small, ancient dam breached by a waterfall that filled a crystal pool at its base. Boy plunged in first, I followed, and we came up on the other bank. We then headed back downstream, clambering atop the larger boulders along the way. Boy tossed rocks into the water just to hear the sound. I watched the light dancing off the rippling water, and saw that I was in mid-stream. All parents are in midstream. My face in the mirror of water reminded me that I'm a salmon who has begun to swim toward the mouth of the river where I was born. So are you. The experience goes by in a flash. Don't waste their time or yours on somebody else's idea of life. If your kid is bugging you, turn off your device or put down your book, even if it's this one, and go out and play.

If you follow these instructions, there will come a time when your kids will give up on you and your crazy world with its incessant cars and dangers and schools and scarce money and rushing around. Congratulations! Their imaginations are working, and pretty soon your kids will have this singular thought, "you poor grownup, trapped as you are in your own thinking, how little you know about the lousy job you have done making this world that you are now foisting upon me. I don't want it. I can do a better job of dreaming up a better way of life over breakfast. Yet you insist on belittling my vision of the world and replacing it with the imaginary world that you have manifested in order to confine me."

So your mission, should you chose to accept it, is to make your kids' real lives as compelling as the gaming, YouTubing, and all the other fake, screen-based nonreality programming that steals their souls. You can complain that it's not fair: it's just you against the phalanx of "content developers" getting paid fat bucks to make reality look boring by comparison. You're also working against evolution, because our species is so easily distracted by new gadgets. Every time something new comes along, we devolve into proto-human apes hooting and jumping around like when we first tamed fire or wielded a bone club. We empty our bank accounts and use up our spare time fiddling with the new gadget. Be aware that making children into zombie consumers has never been easier, and you must liberate yourself before you can liberate them. Make sure that the hand that rocks the cradle is yours, and not the insidious glow from the TV or whatever mini-screen of choice people are bathing their kids in. I just saw a movie, World War Z, in which Brad Pitt plays a former UN worker who has chosen to stay at home with his two kids, but ends up fighting zombies. Pretty close to home. Perhaps the revolution will be televised, after all.

Get Out of My Office

A couple of decent sentences came to me this morning, which these days amounts to a major burst of inspiration, and I was determined to jot them down before they vanished amidst the inevitable interruptions, but the notebook refused to open. Someone had ingeniously fused it shut by firing dozens of high-powered staples through the front and back covers and most of the pages. Then I noticed that the same stapling treatment had been delivered to all of my other notebooks, to my day planner, various paperwork, and huge hunks of blank printer paper. Someone was trying to send me a message: stop writing or else. I ignored the threat, but lived to regret my false bravado when my computer mysteriously fell off my desk soon afterwards, crashing the hard drive and wiping my slate clean. I have tried keeping the marauders out of the workspace by bellowing "get out of my office!" more times than any harried middle-manager, which is amazing considering that I only manage two people.

These two critters have simplified my work life better than any highly paid professional organizer. I no longer initiate or return phone calls because they repurposed my address book as a coloring book. I no longer worry about organizing files because they have disappeared. I no longer worry about works in progress, because they have been deleted. My once well-organized home office has devolved into a post-apocalyptic scene due to their various feats of monkey-wrenching, such as when Girl strutted up to me today and proudly announced, "I cleaned it with my spit!" Oh really--you cleaned what? "Everything! I rubbed it in!" She showed me the walls, desk, and my laptop, for starters. A three year-old with over-active salivary glands had spit-shined my entire office, or should I say, spit-smeared it. She scattered my pens and papers all over the house, and although it makes me mad, I'm also chagrined by the fact that she uses them to write, illustrate, and produce books by the dozen. "Dad," she asked, "I wrote three books today. You're a writer. How many did you write?" Well, umm.

Still, when a call comes in from an old friend with an urgent project, I occasionally get sucked back into the UN orbit. As soon as that happens, and I'm on the line with some Undersecretary General or Ambassador, Boy likes to pick up one of the phone extensions and emit a combination of heavy breathing and incoherent mumbling. He never bothers to produce such sound effects when I speak with lower level functionaries. The call will then be terminated when he accidentally autodials another number. The kids also know that important phone calls are ripe opportunities for hijinx in other rooms, like dispatching a one pound bottle of honey with chopsticks, covering their entire bodies with liquid soap, or climbing atop the kitchen counter to attack the child-proof top on the vitamin bottle. They enjoy making me choose between trying to save the world and trying to save them.

The bottom line is that if you try to work in a home office while also caring for young children, their constant interruptions will prevent you from writing or reading or thinking, unless it's thinking about their need to play or eat or fight with their sibling. You must accept the fact that their overall growth will be fed by your overall decline. One way to counteract the early onset of dementia is to develop a case of what I call the Addams disorder, named after Charles Addams, the cartoonist who created the Adams Family. Charlie was an alchemist who inverted the ideal of a perfect family, and thereby saved their sanity. The Addams Disorder begins with the creative destruction of your carefully organized sense of order. Let kids wreck your world, at least halfway, so that you can rethink your place in it. Your idea of what it means to work at home should be the first to go. On this job, working at home is equivalent to being the sole employee of a restaurant, a laundromat, a visiting nurse service, a tutoring service, a buying club, a landscaping company, a pocket zoo, a life coaching service, and a school for manners, all simultaneously on a 24 hour 7 day a week basis with no days off and no pay whatsoever. This stark reality means that you must get used to a lot of other things going completely to hell around you. Things will not work out if your partner is a neat freak. Like the character of Mortitia, they should embrace a sensibility that considers the bizarre to be somewhat normal. The partner of a SAHD needs to be at least as iconoclastic as the SAHD himself. If you learn to embrace your inner Gomez and she embraces her inner Mortitia, you might have a shot at making the arrangement work.

The Look that Knows Better

The playground is a surprisingly fruitful arena for the exploration of sexual politics. Putting aside for a moment the fact that you'll often be the only parent there, (the other grownups being indentured servants airlifted from foreign backwaters), the majority of actual mothers that you'll encounter in playgrounds will welcome your presence. However, a certain few will react as though you pose a multivalent threat: you are in their environment, doing their job, yet you are not one of them. They will glare at you out of the corners of their eyes, beaming an acrid combination of suspicion, resentment, and confusion. Most SAHDs know this scalding glance so well that they can imitate it with hilarious precision. It says *"go away.* Stop threatening my job, my marriage, my role in life, my raison d'etre! Never mind that you have brought your own two kids with you, I will assume that you are a pedophile on the prowl in the hope it will shame you into leaving this hallowed ground."

Luckily, I have no shame left to manipulate, and am thus able to explore the various reasons why I've become a barometer of female self-confidence. Those mothers who are most comfortable with themselves are the most likely to enjoy my presence, while those who are the least self-assured find it so intolerable that they must attempt to expel me from their domain. One way to preempt their effort is to call out "stranger danger!" before they do.

When I was first promoted to this position about 10 years ago, (Exec. V.P., Ass Wiping Division), I sensed that some moms saw me as the new hire, or worse, a scab who crossed the gender role line, and threatened to unseat them from life-long employment. The requisite job skills are not easily transferable, unless you hope to follow the Dickensonian business plan of opening a foster home and picking over the bones of various welfare agencies. Every SAHD or MAHD out there has been struck by this chilling epiphany: your future earning potential and job prospects diminish with every minute you spend running a household. Maybe that's why certain MAHDs feel insecure. Good reason, actually.

Another possible reason for the unfriendly mother syndrome may be that they fear the idea of societal upset due to sex in the workplace if men flood this particular job market. You'd have men and women, who are not partners, comingling all day in close proximity to empty bedrooms. On the other hand, the likelihood of sex actually occurring is greatly diminished due to caretakers being surrounded by the alarming products of such couplings. They are literally in your face all the time. Do we really want more of this torture? Such a strong disincentive to further couplings cannot be ignored. But let's imagine for a moment that natural urges overwhelm the countervailing restraints, and play leaps like wildfire from the playground to the bedroom. We'd quickly turn into a gigantic tribe of people with uncertain parentage, sort of like the Screen Actor's Guild. Some MAHDs recoil in horror at the prospect of such a chaotic future scenario, which is augured by your presence in the playground.

Allow me to put those mothers' fears to rest, though, by pointing out that intergenerational female solidarity has a way of eliminating the possibilities discussed in the foregoing. For instance, my Girl instinctively serves as her mother's eyes and ears in the field. I once had a neighbor, let's call her Sally, who was a very pretty young mother. While my Girl had a playdate with her Girl, I would usually spend a few minutes talking with Sally. Afterwards, my Girl always carefully reported these interactions back to Wife as soon as she thought I safely out of earshot. "Dada and Sally were talking and talking and looking and looking!" she'd say. Girl knew that Sally posed an existential threat, and she was going to disarm it before it went nuclear. She remained in cahoots with her mother to ensure that their mutual interest—my sole allegiance—would be protected through careful and continuous monitoring for signs of trouble. Of course, things never went further with Sally, otherwise I wouldn't be writing these words, or perhaps even breathing this breath. So all of you SAHDs out there, be forewarned: if you have a Girl, she will be your Wife's watchdog.

As a group, we men may need to mature a bit before we're ready to take the helm of the future. It's just too difficult to take care of a baby when you're a big baby yourself. Luckily, the female of the species keeps civilization motoring forward despite attempts by men to derail it with crack-pot schemes like a SAHD revolution. Remember that the next time you get the look that thinks it knows better.

Do What I Say And Nobody Gets Hurt

Kids love exploring creative ways to needlessly endanger their lives and limbs. Slamming car doors on each other is such fun for children of a certain age. The way they figure it, who really needs ten fingers? Keep all ten and you're bound for piano lessons. Better to endure a brief moment of pain now than to suffer through a decade of tedium under the tutelage of a failed and embittered musician. (Of course, no teacher we've ever had fits that description). Here's another hilarious gag: go ahead and see how many pennies you can stuff into your mouth. Can you top it off with a Sacagewa dollar? How about a super ball—its just the perfect size to clog a windpipe! There is such fun to be had with simple household items. Try stuffing tissues into a toaster and see what happens. Of course, the irony of liking what can kill them until it finally does applies to many adults, too. But fathers who are child caretakers are not granted the luxury of such stupid behavior, for we exist primarily to protect our

89

children from every evil that awaits them. We're designed by nature to be expendable, willing and eager to exchange our life for the survival of our offspring or those closest to us. Politicians have long exploited this instinct to keep their war machines humming. But I digress.

Yelling at kids to stop doing whatever obviously life-threatening thing they're doing is useless. Danger is such irresistible fun for them that you must physically intervene. Hence, the essential work of parenting is lifeguarding. So from now on, I will refer to the performance of childcare duties as being "on the job" as a tribute to my father, who was an NYPD detective. Being "on the job" was shorthand used by cops who wore plain clothes to identify each other. We SAHDs are like plain clothes lifeguards, out of uniform, but on the job.

On a summer break from college, I had been a County Lifeguard at a place in New York where on any given Sunday we'd have 7,000 people on the beach and another 2,000 in the adjacent pool. Whole families would put themselves in ridiculous danger because they knew I was supposed to be watching them. As a lifeguard, your job is to let people be adventurous while also being ready to save their asses. It's a fine line to walk, and excellent practice for parenting. Both jobs require you to withstand hours of boredom punctuated by moments of sheer terror. Although you try to be constantly watchful, those moments usually strike at the nanosecond during which your attention has lapsed, or your gaze diverted by some external stimuli, such as a florescent pink string bikini. It will be during your glance away from the water that some person will be transformed into nothing more than bubbles bursting at the surface. It's the same at the playground, where during your glance away from your kid, they will suddenly be transformed into a body falling through space. I have made more than one diving save to catch my daughter as she rolled off various play sets. Perhaps I'm just some former public safety officer with Post Traumatic Stress Disorder who can't stop replaying old routines. I suppose I should get counseling, fulltime babysitting, and a "real job." I pledge to absolutely do that, starting right away in the next life.

One note of warning before taking precautions intended to make your kids safer: you might find yourself subject to the mysterious ironies that are always at work, and discover that you've accidentally increased the hazard quotient exponentially. Like the time I cut some saplings in the yard as low to the ground as possible so there wouldn't be any pungi sticks set like backyard booby traps. Then I redoubled my efforts and covered what was left with heaps of pine combs. My mind had not grasped how those pine comb mounds were perfect for a toddler looking to practice his log rolling skills. Boy got atop a pile and began joyously running in place while the combs rolled underfoot. It was like a tiny treadmill, until he reached all the way to the ground and tripped, falling face down right onto one of those low, sharp sapling trunks. It punctured his cheek to the bone, missing his eye by less than an inch. The scar he will carry throughout his life is a reminder that my best efforts are sometimes worse than no effort at all.

While I'm in a confessional mood and on the topic of safety, I must admit that I nearly killed my entire family once, except I did it the old fashioned way—with a car. We drove out to Amish country on a spring afternoon to visit the gatherings called "mud sales." These are great places to buy a horse-drawn buggy or imagine that you're living in a previous century. On streets surrounding the sales, families have garage sales with clothing so neatly arranged you'd think that you were visiting a Ralph Lauren store, minus the officious sales help. One such sale caught my eye, and I decided to quickly check it out. I backed up the driveway, which was pitched slightly downward, toward a busy county road. I didn't want to deal with unbuckling car seat carriers and wrestling with overly willful tiny people, so I jumped out alone, but in my rush, I forgot just one thing: to put the car into park. With all souls aboard, the Camry started rolling down the driveway towards the street where cars were flashing by in a high-speed stream from both directions. I sprinted toward the car with the terrible knowledge that everything depended upon my reaching it before it rolled out into that road. At the last minute, I managed to leap into the driver's seat and jam on the brakes. No matter what hassles are swirling around you and no matter how they are impinging on your goals, a SAHD must develop a kind of patience that does not come naturally to most men.

Even if you're willing to die to keep your kids safe, there are countless ways to lose them once and forever. Every lifeguard knows that there are many situations beyond your control. Someone can have a heart attack and disappear beneath the waves. A shark can gobble up a top swimmer. A rip current can send a mass of people out to sea all at once. Personally, I never believed half the stuff I heard in church, or in the strange book that supposedly held the secrets of life. But now that I'm running around trying to keep kids safe from invisible ticks and solar rays and SUVs, I can see why religions got such traction in the first place. They were created by parents as a way to beseech the great mystery to protect their progeny. Kids are the real reason for religion, and raising them is a religious experience, complete with glimpses of heaven and hell.

I came to this realization at the end of one particularly stressful day. My back ached, my head pounded, and my nerves were so shredded that I thought any work outside of the house would be better than continuing the living hell of being a SAHD sack. That night, I dreamt of losing Girl. The nightmare brought a singular clarity to my work. No activity in this life can compare with the importance of safeguarding a child. The rest is bunk. This book is bunk. Put it down now and go do something for your kid. You're not a SAHD, or a butt-wiper. You're a lifeguard, and you're on duty.

To Sleep and Sleep Not

One morning in the very near future, you will step bleary-eyed out of bed and hear a slow, mournful dirge emanating from the lower reaches of hell. No, you have not awakened to find yourself in a David Lynch movie, as you've always feared. You have merely disturbed a motion-activated toy that is bewailing its dying battery by moaning a nursery rhyme in slow motion. As the noise runs down pitifully, it will strike you as a fitting soundtrack to your state of mind. That's because you have not slept properly in a decade. Even worse, you're probably now in a broken sleep pattern that will last for the rest of your natural life. Upon reaching the bathroom, the mirror will greet you with eyes that are sinking deeper into their black-rimmed sockets with each passing day. Your fuse will be very short already, and getting progressively shorter as the day wears on until you finally explode, probably just before you serve dinner, but certainly no later than the imbroglio commonly known as kids' teeth-brushing time.

Welcome to sleep deprivation, the unsung villain of parenthood and the final factor that turns this job into a sustained combat situation.

Medical researchers are now associating sleep deprivation with every bad thing from Alzheimer's disease to obesity. Yet no doctor wants to look at the underlying reason and blame it on the kids. Luckily, I'm here and happy to do so. For the first couple of years of childcare, they will need to have their diapers changed multiple times throughout the night. Right around the time you've got them potty trained, they will begin dreaming, and all of their dreams will be nightmares, perhaps because you are the one taking care of them during the daytime. The horrified screaming usually begins around midnight, and can last for over an hour, which wakes up the other child. Things cascade from there until the sun rises without your having had the chance to fall back asleep. After some months of this torture, you will let them take refuge in your bed when they have night terrors. They will fall asleep immediately, but then begin muttering, snorting and twitching their way through all kinds of remembered dramas of the day. They will sleep but you will not. If you have multiple kids, your state of sleep-deprivation will continue seamlessly until you become a monster in waking life. This is where people go bad.

The lifeguarding duties of a SAHD extend to guarding the sleep of the money-earner. If you didn't handle all manner of overnight emergencies, including protecting your partner from the demons that your kids encounter in their dreams, she might become sleep-deprived too, and bite her boss's head off one day, which is generally frowned upon in most workplaces outside the UFC cage. You are the only parent who can be sleep deprived, because your children cannot fire you, at least not as of this writing, although with the state trying to horn in on nanny duties, I cannot guarantee that your little charges will not be able to fire you by the time you read this entry. So whoever is in charge at home during the day must also stay on duty throughout the night. The bad math equation now reads 24/7/365. You must also suffer the added insult of getting chastised by the well-slept money-earner for appearing short-tempered with the children during those brief moments when the money-earner graces the family with their presence before fleeing back to the world of grownups. Remain steadfast in your position as the midnight prowler and the daytime growler. You will begin to catch up on your sleep when the youngest one turns eight.

My Kryptonite

Note to Lex Luthor: we have discovered the only thing that can defeat Super Dad. Apply the high-pitched howling of a girl toddler who is crying like the world is coming to an end to both of his ears first thing in the morning, preferably inside a tiled bathroom. The relentless, piercing screaming will ricochet at Super Dad from all directions, send his brain chemistry into chaos, and knife into the deepest recesses of his soul. First he will become confused, then appear to be the agony, and finally, the air will become like a soup that he must swim through on his way to becoming catatonic and defenseless. At that point, he will be putty in your hands.

Spy agencies worldwide have long used sound torture to break prisoners without leaving an external mark on their bodies. It's a ruthless technique originally invented by children to bring Super Moms to heel. Therefore, Super Dads need only small doses before they lose whatever relatively feeble powers they possessed to begin with. Once again, evil can then run rampant.

Don't get me wrong. Girl is the sweetest, most precious being in the world. Except when she's howling like a Banshee clamped to my leg while I'm trying to cook dinner--a chore already fraught with challenges for me. As illuminated previously, men have internal chemical allies always at the ready because we're designed to protect our families come what may, and Girl's blood-curdling screams send adrenaline bursting through my arteries. Although she's never in danger when she cries, my chemical response automatically happens anyway, aging my whole system and reminding me just how ill-adapted I am to handling the job of child caretaker. False alarms being rung constantly can put a man in his grave. The hormones must be flushed out of your system by exercise, or they will ruin it. Kids will kill you, if you let them, and if you let them kill you, you will be a very bad parent indeed—an absent one.

Take heart, Super Dads: I've discovered a lead shield that can protect you from this kryptonic, sonic assault. The distillation of everything I know about this job--the single most valuable nugget of parenting advice that I can offer--is to get several sets of earplugs and keep them handy throughout the house. These little foam wonders are the single most important pieces of child paraphernalia you can own. Earplugs not only protect you from the onslaught of blood curdling screams, miserable crying, and high decibel screeching, but also from your own yelling. Marvelous inventions! I keep my primary set at the ready in a little baby bowl right atop the fridge. Equip yourself thusly, and you too will be able to blithely sing along with Chrissy Hynde at those otherwise desperate moments: *it is time, for you to stop, all of your crying.*

Still, you must beware that although these lead shields might work for you, they do nothing for others who are within shouting distance. That will cause you some trouble, such as the time a middle aged woman screamed right back at Girl during a flight, or the time we visited the Metropolitan Museum of Art, where for over an hour I had been straining to keep Girl and the priceless art safely apart. Toward the end of our visit, she needed to go to the bathroom, so I took her in, where she sat but didn't bother to go. Perhaps she was expecting to view some special art in that special room. If so, she managed to hold her disappointment in check, until I prevented her from playing in the sink. The ensuing meltdown was a monumental show of human emotion.

I managed to get Girl out of the restroom, but Wife chose to ratchet up the volume by insisting that she go back in there to pee before we left. That sounded reasonable, but once inside, she still didn't have to go. Instead, she dropped down onto the filthy floor of the stall, and I committed the sin of not letting her crawl over into the next stall, which proved to be the kicker. She started hollering in earnest, and I had to hold onto her harder than if I'd a 40 pound tarpin on the line. I pried her out of the stall and took her outside, where she arched her back and continued screaming at the top of her lungs. The otherwise placid halls of culture reverberated with a painful wail that brought mute stares of pity from the throng of passer-bys. Wife and Boy were on their own bathroom break for what seemed an eternity. There was nothing I could do but return the stares of all those strangers with a hapless, helpless look. In desperation, I tried putting Girl down so she could cry in a corner or against the wall instead of down the halls, but she would have none of it. She grabbed and held onto my collar with all of her toddler super-strength. Exorcism to be seemed the only option. The Power of Christ Commands You!

A museum guard approached approached, and I steeled myself for the indignity of being thrown out of the MET. Instead, he said that he must also deal with the same challenge at home every morning when his daughter bawls her heart out over clothing conflicts. At least I let Girl cry all she wants over garment choices in the hope that she's getting all her image anxiety out of the way now, and by adolescence, she'll be an intellectual who sees through the fashion business. You see, I, too, have a dream.

Another health hazard related to crying and weeping, but one that unfolds more slowly, is the act of eating dinner with people who are melting down in their chairs every night. After enduring such a gut-wrenching meal, one feels vaguely ill. After a few weeks of that torture, one feels mentally rattled. After a few months, one's sanity ebbs away, slowly but surely, like a spring tide. Well paid men in white lab coats have invented drug product lines especially for people who have endured, and must continue to endure, such treatment at the hands of little people.

Hold it! I cannot write this word without interruption. Must…get…earplugs… in! Okay, they're tightly fitted to my ear canal. Now, where was I?

The Big T

And now for the bad news: raising kids will chemically castrate you. A recent study has shown that men who care for children undergo a lowering of their testosterone levels. So if you find yourself on the job, get ready to not only be *considered* less of a man, but to actually *be* less of a man. Are you man enough for that? Don't believe me? Ask your friendly neighborhood endocrinologist. Encroaching eunuch-hood is just another hazard that comes with the territory of this challenge to mind, body, and spirit. Forget ultimate fighting, jousting, or bow hunting for wild boar. If you want to test your manhood, give up everything and take solo care of multiple children with at least one still in diapers. Then we'll see who's the toughest of them all.

The physiological process is quite simple. Your male hormones are rendered superfluous by the very nature of the job. Instead of battling Viking raiders and hunting the Irish elk into extinction,

I'm cuddling a three year-old, applying Destin cream to the diaper rash on a one year old, all while worrying whether I made the oatmeal soft enough so that I won't have to perform a mini-Heimlich maneuver. As a result, my boy hormones are not only dispensable, they're actually a barrier to mustering the patience and gentle touch required to accomplish the job at hand. So the body, in its infinite wisdom, is slowly jettisoning them. I can now see why SUVs become so popular. These macho-looking machines were marketed specifically to men who're desperately seeking to compensate for the precipitous drop in their T levels. Brilliantly done to us once again, Madison Ave! Could our eager adoption of all technology be compensatory for an overall drop in T amongst the male population correlative with the advance of civilization? Perhaps, but for now I'll stick to what my body is telling me, and it's telling me that I need a nap.

We can, however, speculate on the reasons why evolution would favor the phenomenon of T-drop among caretakers. Lower levels might reduce a man's likelihood to exchange phone numbers with that gorgeous Icelandic Au Pair at the playground, leaving the child fatherless and less likely to pass on their own genes. My theory says that the Big T gives us the strength and impulsiveness to risk our lives to save a child in extreme danger, but it also puts that same child in extreme danger should we have to care for them day in and day out over a period of years. Just one moment of too much force and we're talking infanticide.

Once again, nature figured out a survival strategy: tweak down the level of the hormone that makes men testy. The funny thing is that most men are too weak to clean up poop, pee, and puke amidst howling cries every day and night for years on end. They're too concerned about their manhoods to wash half a dozen plastic pants and hang them out to dry. So here we have uncovered yet another paradox at work: on this job, strength is weakness, and weakness is strength. Lower T levels also correlate with lower levels of prostate cancer. So my kids might be saving my life, even as they threaten my life as I had known it.

Wait a minute—I've had another epiphany!

Men who are caring for their kids have a higher baseline level of testosterone. They're aggressive soccer players, big-boned marathoners, hirsute weightlifters, and former commercial divers. They are not the types who hire landscaping services or don't own a snow shovel. By becoming SAHDs, they're self-medicating. Child care lowers their T levels back down into the normal range, allowing them to fit in better with society, even as they're becoming misfits once again: SAHDs in a MAHD world. That's the ticket! We're actually supermen, brought to heel by strange, wee little people. High flyers who've taken a voluntary dive. Men with masculinity to spare. Yes, I like that image. I had too much T, and so my subconscious chose to regulate those restless hormones by steering me into this profession, which is truly the world's oldest. At least I fit the description in this one sense--if I cared about what people think, I'd be in trouble. That could be a sign of high T or low IQ. Take your pick. So I must limp along, (figuratively only, I assure you) on lower T levels than I was programmed to enjoy. So what if I need a nap now and then? So did Einstein, I think it was.

Now you're really scared, right? Coward! You must take eunuch-hood like a badge of honor, signifying things hard-lost, so to speak. Don't worry, you can always try to offset the T drain by taking up bull riding, big wave surfing, or mud running, that is, if you're not feeling too punked-out to even get up off the couch. It all comes down to one simple question that you must ask yourself before following my humble path: am I man enough to be a mother? We shall see.

What Did You Do In The War, Daddy?

The Pentagon reports that a soldier loses 100% of his fighting effectiveness after 60 days of battle. Yet it takes over 900 days to get a kid to the point where they'll stop constantly endangering their own lives at all hours of the day and night. As elucidated in a preceding entry, you'll also endure continual bombardment by a fiendish mix of screaming, full-throated hollering, high-pitched screeching, and wailing mixed with relentless badgering during those 3 or 4 years of battle. For this and much, much more, you will love them more than anything on Earth. But let's save that part for later.

For now, you'll find that battle fatigue manifests itself first in a selective form of neural pruning. Five years of building children's vocabularies have left me unable to call up words like, *implications*. I've siphoned down my pool of words to fill up theirs', and the implications, especially for a writer, are worrisome. Polysyllabic words and proper nouns often escape me, with the word "things" becoming a multipurpose stand-in. Other times, I find myself using whole sentences to describe an idea that should have been articulated by a single word. I often get the urge to write poetry that sings to the heart of existence, but instead I must wash dishes to the wails of a tormented 3 year-old girl whose brother enjoys and encourages any emotionally wrenching display. If they are indeed sparing my prostate, they're sacrificing my brain in the bargain. I once tried a simple trip to the local planetarium, trying to expand their little minds, and ended up with mine so shrunken from stress that I can barely remember the word, *planetarium*.

The real worry is whether or not I am stuck at this lower level of intellectual functioning for the rest of my natural life. It's not like I could afford that much off to begin with. Doing the other jobs I do might have partially salvaged my neural capacities, or not, since I wouldn't be able to judge, would I? These activities, (I almost wrote "things"), such as renovating the houses we've lived in, consulting for the U.N., or tackling various writing projects, also added to the overall stress levels, so it's probably a wash. My wife the brain scientist thinks that I've been sliding into dementia since we met 20 years ago. Then again, she also thought I was going deaf, and sent me off to an audiologist for a hearing check-up. My hearing is fine, but it has become selective, which is a skill that gets sharpened every day one cares for children. You've got to block out the noise or go nuts. I can identify fake cries coming from another room and block them out, sometimes to the horror of female visitors who think I'm being criminally neglectful. My brain filters loud crashes or otherwise dire sounds as long as there's no telltale yelping, proving to me that the old noggin is as active as it always was, just in different ways. Unfortunately, these ways not useful for anything but raising kids.

For instance, I now know that it isn't necessarily loud crashes that signify trouble. Deafening silence in the house can offer a much more telltale warning. This afternoon while having a corrective talk with boy, I let Girl slip away for a moment before hearing that scary silence in the rest of the house. I jumped up and hurried from room to room, but she was nowhere to be found. Then I discovered a gooey white substance spread all over the floor of her room, sticking the pillow to the sheets, the sheets to the blanket, and the blanket to the bed. It ran up the walls and down onto the rug where it lay in a thick pool. I followed the white trail on the floor into her brother's room and up into his bed. I pulled back the covers and discovered her there, huddling naked, her entire body and hair covered in a huge mass of the goopy white stuff. She would not reveal it's origin or composition, so I had to do the taste test. It was not toothpaste, as was the case yesterday, but good old Elmer's Glue-All, finally living up to its name. She had climbed high onto my desk to get at two brand new super giant sized bottles, and raced upstairs to glue her world back together into its primordial state of unified grace.

There are times on this job when you must simultaneously wash humans and their abodes at the same time with the fury of an indoor thunderstorm. At those times, your sanity will thank me for suggesting that you keep a cache of small baby sized washcloths at the ready. With them, I have the tools needed to take corrective action. Without them, all would be lost. To the ladies out there, I know that this is common sense, but believe me, it represents a cognitive leap for most of us men.

The next day, things were alarmingly quiet again. I rose and discovered another trail, this time of flour, which I followed along the floor from the kitchen, through the living room, to a dead-end behind the couch. Both kids were perched on a giant pile of flour and beans that had a box of staples mixed in for extra zing. "We're cooking!" they said as they dumped in a carton of milk. They were so proud of their new concoction that kicking and screaming ensued when physical extraction of their persons became necessary. The smell of bad news in Girl's pants put an end to any fanciful ideas of writing even a few lines today, after all. Tomorrow will be no different, but remember that this is a marathon, and in a decade, things shall reverse themselves, and your adolescents will bid you to leave them alone.

In addition to the potential for insults to your brain, there are other hidden dangers lurking for the unsuspecting SAHD. Consider yourself on notice that playgrounds are deceptively perilous places for over-confident middle-aged males. Just last week, some baseball star wrecked his career while attempting to play in one. His millions evaporated when he did something stupid that caused a hideous ankle injury. During all the years I've spent inside playgrounds, I've never once seen a child or a woman get seriously hurt. That's because women are smart enough to not leap around—only fathers do that when trying to get some exercise, and they wind up in the ER. I was almost one of them. One day, I found myself standing atop a 5 ft. platform while my toddler began climbing a ladder up to meet me. The likelihood of her slipping off the ladder was greater than you might imagine since she was wearing a corrective hip brace. It dawned on me that if she fell, I would be unable to catch her, and so I jumped out over her onto the ground, then turned to spot her from beneath. Such a move would not have been any problem in my 20s, but when I landed in my 40s, the impact tore something in my knee. Girl made it to the top just fine, but for me playtime was over. I hobbled away, pushing the baby stroller that now served double duty as a walker, while several

Caribbean nannies righteously mocked me for being such an idiot.

Perhaps the problem lies in the way that men have slyly compressed all definitions of heroism into a few manageable minutes, or at most, a few hours of elapsed real time, during which we perform foolish deeds to earn the laurels and medals that will prove our courage to others, and hopefully, to ourselves. In the grandiose male view, heroics performed quickly generate the brightest blaze of glory. Take out an enemy machine gun nest, save someone who's fallen onto the subway tracks, snatch a child from a burning house, or take a bullet for the president. With this strategy, we've effectively stolen the thunder of real sacrifice, the kind that is endured over years and decades--the kind that has been lived by women since we decided there was little celebrity or fun to be garnered by corralling kids and keeping them safe and fed all day and night. What about the authentic heroism of the day-to-day labors of unpaid, inglorious, and often unsatisfying child care duties that grind down body, mind, and spirit? This ultimate valor unfolds in slow motion, and there are no medals given out for it, no parades launched, no audiences with the President, and of course, no service related disability payments.

Childcare is a long twilight struggle, a hot war that threatens to turn cold, then hot, then cold again, and will only be truly over when you meet your own ignominious end.

No matter what the Marines would have us believe, tough guys are too damned fragile to handle the ultra-marathon of child rearing, especially not with the crowds of people who are booing you from both sides all along the route. A man who's keeping house with children? There must be something wrong with him! After all, we need our money. We need our beer and food. We need our exercise. We need our quiet. We need to win. We need our intellectual and professional fulfillment. We need our self-regard bolstered at every turn. We are so damned needy that we've enslaved the other half of our species to work for us, and to support us in all the fundamental ways. Who cares if we need to go off and fight a jolly war now and then to prove that we're essential? So here's a toast to what Daddy did in the war. I took care of you, you little bugger, and your wild little sister.

The Big E

Out of fear and respect, the word Estrogen should always be capitalized. There is no bigger "E" word in the known universe. This mysterious molecule drives women to do some very strange things in the months after they give birth to children. They will roam the streets with tears streaming down their cheeks if the dog has escaped from the yard. With alarming regularity, they'll walk out of the house with no intention of ever returning, until 10 minutes later. They'll throw wild, end-of-the-world tantrums if you say the slightest thing wrong, only to break down in a teary mess when they return to their senses. You'll pay a high price for these emotional bonfires, which are all fed by that highly combustible hormone, Big E.

Thanks to being blessed and cursed with E, women possess the superior strength necessary to perform the job of raising children. They have great fun letting us think that we live in a patriarchy, but in fact, E rules. Just ask any torturer and he'll tell you: a man will break long before a woman. Coining the term "the weaker sex" amounted to another brilliantly fallacious public relations spin job, for the sad fact is that men are the weaker sex. All of our strutting and fretting in the workplace is child's play compared to a MAHD's job. We need constant accolades to bolster our fragile egos, an inflated sense of self and net worth, and enough time to paint on cave walls. People who take care of children don't have the time pursue these false gods. Tasks essential to the continuance of life need to get done, and get done now, regardless of whether anyone else agrees. During the thousands of years that men have been sitting around philosophizing, making masks, dancing around fires and scheming up criminal enterprises, women have been saving our species from extinction by feeding, watching, and cleaning up the next generation. There's no money in it. No awards. No travel. No power. Why do they do it? The answer might lie in a brief examination of the wonderful and wicked world of Big E.

Everyone knows that ladies have some serious hormonal shifts to contend with, or should I say, for us all to contend with. It's hard for men to keep up when we're dealing with Mother Teresa one day and Margaret Thatcher the next, depending upon lunar and tidal transits. Their worldview is not warped by our deranged concepts of absolute beginnings and endings. Life for them is cyclical. Maybe that's why the prospect of death doesn't worry them quite so much as it worries us. Men are not really capable of imagining how it must feel to have the life-giving power of the universe flowing through your veins. We SAHDs feel lucky to have enough juice in there to get us to the weekend.

Estrogen's power is revealed when it finally begins to ebb, and women are thrown into a state of transformation that can get tough on everyone around them. Even the word we've given it—menopause--sounds like they're taking break, or a time-out, (from men, perhaps?). Don't think of letting an unkind word escape from your mouth during this particular time in a woman's life. I know this not from observing my Wife, who has yet to hit menopause, but from my mother, who wrestled with that demon for years before things quieted down. To balance out the disparity between her and her five large athletic sons, she liked to transform innocuous household items into weapons of mass destruction. The balance of power between T and E, even if it was ebbing, was never in doubt. On the other hand, her three beautiful daughters posed a different, more metaphysical conundrum. They were already attracting too many suitors, and like all girls of that age, were drawn to fun-loving losers. Mom didn't know how to control them, so she gave that one up to God, which meant they'd have to learn the hard way and hopefully come out alive.

The mythological character, Sisyphus, condemned to spend eternity rolling a boulder up a mountainside everyday, only to have it roll back down every night, was clearly invented by a woman in charge of cooking and caring for a large family. On my mother's last night, I told her that she'd done it: successfully raised eight kids. "I thought it was never going to end," she admitted. Sisyphus was no sissy. They should have made him a woman, because he exhibited the kind of fortitude that one needs on the ultra-marathon of child-raising. Women do things like swim for 4 days from Cuba to Key West while fending off sharks and getting stung by jellyfish until their lips bleed. No man would attempt such a feat. Yet several women have tried, some more than once, and two have actually made it all the way. We men cannot match such endurance because we lack the secret ingredient that has been optimized specifically for long haul endeavors after millions of years of evolution. The Big E. It's why women are so strong, and why we've had to oppress them all these years.

Most men are just too damn weak to raise children. We'd rather run around in search of confirmation that we do in fact exist, and that we will not die. So who again is the weaker sex? It's Big E's world. We just live in it.

Father Time

The animal kingdom has certain members, such as salmon, who completely escape childcare duties by checking out before their kids check-in. They live, love, and then promptly die. There is no more elegant solution to the age-old problem of how to evade the task to which this book is dedicated. If we consider celebrities to be their own kettle of fish, we have found the salmon of the human experience. To name just a few of that species with the money and much younger women to sire kids after their 50th, 60th, or even 70th winter, take a look at John Travolta, Michael Douglas, Dennis Quaid, Nick Nolte, Bruce Willis, Woody Allen, Kevin Costner, and David Letterman. I recall seeing a photo of the actor Tony Randall beaming and holding his new baby in a sling. The only problem was that he was 80 at the time, and he did not survive the ordeal. If you wait that long to have a kid, nature will consider your job of procreation done, and she shall usher you into the next life post haste. Older dads make better dads, up to a point, but the job is definitely not for the geriatric set.

In my case, the world kept me busy until I was ready for kids at around 36, but as I discussed earlier, my wife wasn't ready. Her education as a scientist was dragging on forever, and she didn't want it derailed by pregnancy. So we waited. My mother began to show her impatience by giving meaningful gifts. One Christmas it was a clock with birds on it, and the next, an outdoor thermometer with bees on it. When I pointed out the recurring motif of reproductive symbolism on her gifts, she threatened to go further: "just wait until you see what I'm going to give you next year!" We conceived a child immediately rather than find out.

If you've fathered children in your 40s or beyond, you've got to stop worrying and learn to love your inner geezer, because doing the actuarial math can make things look a bit grim. The calculations on my older kid look okay, but my younger one will graduate high school when I'm 63, and college at 66. If I'm lucky enough to still be live at 75, she'll be only 30. I could be 80 before I get the chance to hold a grandchild, which should absolve me from diaper duty, though probably not.

The Daily News printed a picture of old Al Pacino in Central Park, lounging up against a tree while a phalanx of attendants swarmed his baby to change her diaper. It's not so bad being an ancient dad if you can afford that kind of hands-off service. But if you recuse yourself from the job because you have the money to do so, then you're not a real SAHD. You're a ROD, a Rich Old Dad. Being a ROD sure sounds a lot sexier, but you aren't the genuine article, because kids want you to care for their essential needs with your own hands. The simple math of doing so shows that you'll be changing approximately 4 diapers a day for 3 years. That's 365 x 4 x 3, or about 4,400 diapers per kid, which means I've changed close to 9,000 diapers in my career. Pretty impressive stats!

The sweet spot for having kids is probably between 30 and 40. Keep in mind that being on the job means that you'll often be trapped inside, unable to exercise, and surrounded by high-fat foods. When you emerge a decade later, squinting and blinking in the glaring light of a summer day, you might easily resemble those pudgy, pear-shaped characters in *Tell-A-Tubbies*. If you're a fortyish man, you'd better get moving, because let me tell you, Tinky Winky, that after the magical age of fifty, there's a good chance that having a baby in the house will kill you.

Perhaps the best solution to the epidemic of old Dads, and to overpopulation in general, would be for men to get sterilized around the time that women go into menopause. In my vision of a better world, I see a commercial van with a big red "V" (for

Vasectomy) careening up to your door on or about your 50th birthday. Strong men wearing red uniforms would jump out, followed by a delicate lass dressed in surgical garb. She would move with deliberate grace and confidence up to the apartment door. At the ring of the doorbell, the male inhabitant, knowing what awaits, would either go resignedly to his fate, or run like the devil. What he does not know is that the V team is equipped for any challenge. The poor runner would be subdued, since our valiant employees of the state would be recruited from the ranks of inner city track stars and wrestlers now enjoying decent paying jobs, even if the specific details of those jobs may be somewhat indecent.

Once the aging lothario is immobilized, the woman's skilled hands would go to work, and in no time, a new man would emerge, his aging sperm forever retired, and his worries of premature death due to late-onset fatherhood a thing of the past. Society would also be saved from becoming populated with idiots, since once past 50, the age of the father has been correlated negatively with the IQ of the child.

I can hear the pitch now. "Hello, Gates Foundation? I'd like to propose a humanitarian project of global significance: the "V" Corps. Yes. That's "V" for victory. You give us $100 million and we'll save the lives of millions of old farts like your illustrious benefactor. Old white men would be allowed to continue their ignominious rule thanks to the prevention of the distractions and costs associated with ancient fatherhood." I can hear their response now. "Where do we send the check?"

Another Supposedly Helpful Thing I'll Never Do Again

In my endless egotism, I'd like to think that you might want to know something about me, personally, aside from my being on the job. However, my wife thinks not. She prefers to believe that I was born on the night we met, which I find perplexing yet strangely flattering. I'm going to spare this chapter from the knife, and let you decide whether or not you to read about some of the stuff I did that made me crazy enough to think I could handle this solo expedition into the pinnacles and valleys of a SAHD's life.

Ultimately, I blame George Plimpton. He gave me the idea of trying to pack several different lives into a single lifetime. As a kid, the prospect of specializing in one field and following one professional track was too stultifying to consider. Old George was the first person I encountered who did things differently, and although I wanted to emulate him, one crucial aspect of his work escaped me: I had to write about my colorful experiences, not just go out and have them. I tried everything from deep sea diving to opera performing, but never wrote about any of it because my anti-intellectual family never saw the point of all the scribbling done by people who call themselves writers. We were a tribe of oral storytellers who took pleasure in entertaining people in person under a live format. I realized the gap in my plan rather late in the game, but not too late to scribble notes during my SAHD phase. Hence, the book you are now reading.

I started off my adventure by studying marine science, like some kind of Jacques Cousteau from Flatbush Brooklyn, only to wind up becoming a construction worker, albeit underwater. My main problem with getting a job in the environmental field was that mid-career professionals were all losing their jobs right at the time I graduated college. We had a President who said that trees pollute more than cars, and whose first move was to have newly installed solar panels ripped off the White House and thrown into a dumpster. "Dutch" eliminated whole departments that dealt with useless things like fisheries, water resources, and clean air. The country's big slide downward had begun, masked by the rhetoric that it "was morning in America." Mourning, indeed. I gave up all hope and traveled to Northern California, where I would plant redwood saplings on land that had been clear-cut. It turned out to be the toughest job I ever had, physically, other than being a baby wrestler.

The area of the Mendocino Range where I worked had been an ancient forest before being razed by a conglomerate, leaving a tangle of huge fallen trees and massive limbs that some insane statistician considered too small to use. Instead, magnificent Redwoods and Douglas Fir trees were left to rot like the herds of buffalo decimated on the plains a hundred years earlier. My job was to plant hybrid redwood seedlings that would be harvested in forty years by the same rapacious corporation. It paid according to the number of trees I planted, and although I was in the best condition of my life, there was no way to make a livable wage by climbing through the slashed wreckage that covered steep hillsides in search of tiny patches of ground suitable for planting. It is still a mystery to me how the local Pomo Indians managed to do it. Their lines of redwood seedlings would go up and through places that only a Sasquatch could dream of going. By and large, the Pomo were truly hilarious, and we'd have tailgate parties at the end of the day to laugh at the absurdity of the situation. The legal fiction we call a *corporation* had a piece of paper that said it owned land on which the Pomo had lived for thousands of years. The land now looked like a nuclear bomb had been dropped on it, and the Pomo had been reduced to Coolies, picking over the remains. The world had gone all topsy-turvy on them, and that was the saddest/funniest thing imaginable. Nowhere outside of Samuel Beckett's head has humor ever been blacker. The group of us, gathered there in the mud, could not stop laughing.

My next job was at the Peach Bottom nuclear power plant on the banks of the Susquehana River, and it couldn't have been more dangerous and stupid than if I'd robbed the Mob. Inside that gigantic machine, they wanted to replace the old racks that held spent fuel rods, (also known as high-level nuclear waste), with new racks that held more rods, allowing the plant to operate longer and make much more money. The trouble was that these rods give off so much radiation that they're stored at the bottom of 30-foot pools of water called fuel pools. Now, the containment water within every nuclear power plant is the only thing that protects the people of planet Earth from the deadly radiation that generates electricity for our TVs, Christmas lights, and blenders. Inside the dome of a nuclear reactor, there's a space about the size of a concert hall. When you walk out onto the reactor floor, you look down into a circular pool of water 60 feet deep, at the bottom of which you see a cap over the reactor core. The water must be kept crystal clear since anything suspended in that water will become highly radioactive and untouchable for millennia. A giant crane rolls across a beam bisecting the ceiling overhead. The crane's cables reach down into the containment water to lift spent rods out of the reactor and move them through a gate into the fuel pool for storage, all while keeping them submerged, where they will have to stay, continually cooled and kept away from the air, for about a zillion years.

Still, the danger seemed abstract to me, until they used that crane to lift the cap off the reactor core, releasing a super-intense, eerie green blast of light that shot up out of the reactor pool and filled the entire room. To try to imagine that sickly, otherworldly light, think of a glow stick plugged into a trillion watts. Our job was to go into that water in diving gear, with dosimeters attached to our bodies measuring the level of radiation exposure in real time so that the tender could direct you away from the source, while you shackled the fuel rod storage racks so that they could be hoisted out and replaced.

Outside the reactor, things weren't much prettier. The entire structure and the ground surrounding it are made of bomb-proof concrete several feet thick. Tunnels under the concrete funnel water from the river into huge pumps and cooling towers, which keeps the whole crazy machine from destroying the world. The only problem is that these tunnels fill constantly with silt and zebra mussels that threaten to shut down the pumps. So they hoist out concrete manholes 5 feet thick to expose dark brown river water coursing through the tunnels, and ask you to climb down into that water while holding a 3" suction hose attached to an 18-wheeler vacuum tanker truck. In pitch-blackness, I'd feel my way up the tunnel, squishing though the deep ooze that covers the bottom until reaching the pump head. Along the way, there were steel grates to squeeze through, like a set of prison bars set a little too wide, just to make the whole job extra-frightening. Then I'd say, "power on" and begin vacuuming out all several feet of muck laced with sharp mussels. Nice work if you can get it. I lasted long enough to witness the shear lunacy of the nuclear power industry. Little did I know that I'd be headed next to a place that rewarded insanity even more: Wall Street.

I'll make this one short, possibly an *offshore naked short*, although my foray into the world of unbridled greed was far too brief for me to deal in that particular breed of mutant financial instrument. I lasted one month on Beaver Street (don't say it) before realizing that there is no way I can even get out of bed in the morning if my only goal is to make money. How people do it is beyond me. You've got to really worship mammon, or accidentally knock up your girlfriend, to keep at that nonsense. I'd already seen how money had made the world into such a mess, and this experience drove me back to college to try to figure out why.

The main thing I learned studying economics is that people are greedy and scared of dying, and that one feeds the other. I also noticed something else that was very interesting: phone lines could be plugged into PCs, and that simple connection seemed poised to open up something oceanic.

People called it "Videotex" back then. In graduate school, I began writing about the technology's potential, and soon found myself working for a company that had made it big on the French Minitel network, which was a precursor to the internet. I met with many of the major U.S. newspapers and magazines, trying to convince them that that the strange new world of "online services" was their future. The French had gotten there first by handing out little terminals that plugged into the phone line. Their goal was to use it to replace phone books, but they inadvertently triggered a booming new industry when the French, being French, immediately put the technology into the service of love by allowing people to chat and flirt online. Most American publishers couldn't see the future in it, and the newspapers that could were scared to death of losing their classified ad income. Nobody wanted to start an online service, which we now call websites, so I left the French firm and set up my own company in my living room in Styvesant Town. From there, I ran New York City's first online service offering news, email, and classifieds, plus a portal to the French service. The Internet was still years away. The operation held my interest for a year or two, but then things got boring. It was clear that fortunes were going to be made with this technology, but they would be made by very dull people. I suppose that they usually are. Besides, there was this strange new problem looming in the real world, where young New Yorkers had suddenly begun dying in large numbers. Doctors called it the Autoimmune Deficiency Syndrome.

Rumors and disinformation were making everyone panicky, even doctors. Especially doctors. Some media outlets labeled it the "gay plague," but in reality it was taking down all sorts of people, including newborns, old people, and married couples. A federal grant came through my grad school program at NYU, and for the next three years, I got my ersatz medical degree by producing a series of educational programs for the medical community on how to identify and treat the mysterious pandemic. Information was the only cure for it in those days, and it remains the best preventative treatment today. I was finally making enough money to pay the rent by doing work that was worthy of getting out of bed in the morning. Right about the time that the medical community and society at large was beginning to catch up with AIDS, needles began washing up on the beaches of New Jersey.

Back then, cities were still dumping huge barges full of garbage directly into the ocean. I don't know where people thought it would all go, but they were actually surprised when it floated up onto their beaches. It's funny how environmental consciousness expanded overnight after people got worried that they'd step on a needle and get AIDS. Then an environmental conference in Rio de Janeiro drew Presidents from around the world to sign treaties they hoped would address the problems, including the accelerating rate of species extinction, and this other strange one called climate change. Soon afterwards, I got a call from the United Nations. They wanted to funnel some grant money to countries that were trying to find a way out of the mess. For the next ten years, I helped to construct what would become the partnership of UN agencies called the Global Environment

Facility. I took me another ten years of consulting on many other UN initiatives before beginning to wonder whether people who work in glass towers can save the planet.

Now back to The Baby Wrestler.

The Ethics of Elfland

I first encountered legal tender at age 5. My uncle tossed a couple of singles my way that were wretchedly wrinkled from being crumpled up in his pocket. Their talismanic mojo appeared low, and so I went upstairs and ironed them out, hoping to increase their worth by increasing their aesthetic value. They quickly caught fire, and I had to chuck them into the toilet to avoid burning down the house with cash money. That was the last time I had money to burn, but I remember thinking that money is ephemeral, and that the equation adults spouted abouto time=money makes no sense at all. To kids, time=god (god meaning the greatest good), and god=fun. They are born knowing that "deep play" is the philosopher's stone, the Holy Grail, the raison d'etre for the human race. We're here to celebrate life. All the rest amounts to grown-ups getting caught up in their own heads.

The conundrum, then, is how to present the concept of money to children in a way that preempts both destitution on one end, and wealth worship on the other. Some parents try to instill a great respect for money in their children, with little clue that they themselves are ensnared and enslaved by it. I'm inclined to think that these are the kids who will grow up to auction our personal information to the highest bidder, cut back on car safety devices, and do their utmost to sell condo timeshares to captive audiences. On the other hand, one of our greatest fears is to have grown-up children financially dependent upon us because they never grasped the concept of managing their own resources. In the search for a middle ground, it turned out that my kids had more to teach me than I had to teach them.

Children are born with an innate understanding of the elemental truths and tensions that lie beneath the fiction of a cash economy. They'll say things like, "dad, why are you planting grass? You should be planting corn." No adult will ever deliver wisdom like that to a suburban homeowner—it takes a 5 year-old to do it. We should all be planting corn instead of chemical-laden lawns. They're also not afraid to ask, "what would happen if there was no food in the supermarket?" or "how long would it take for everyone to starve if there was no electricity?" or the really big one: "when is God going to let humans go extinct for destroying the world?" Indeed. They're not blind to what has real value, and what is ephemeral, at least not until commercials have had a chance to do their dirty work and confuse their perceptual framework. The longer that parents can help their children hold onto their original concept of what is good and valuable in the world, the better off we'll all be in the future.

One of the hardest realities for a parent to accept is their children's embrace of nonsense, intuition, and the irrational as elements of the highest value, while they reject reason and logic as nearly worthless. They use these values to conjure worlds from their imaginations, which we adults try to drive from them so they can be replaced with the world we have imagined, which consists of videogames, $200 sneakers, and the corporatization of every aspect of life. But we save the really dirty trick for later on, when we tell them that the greatest, most lasting achievements in human history are products of the imagination. We hold up the Bible, the Koran, the Tao Te Ching, the great books and works of art and all the rest. People who held onto their childlike imaginations dreamt up those things. So we rob children of their imaginations, and then show them the immense value of what they've lost. Nice trick on the little buggers! We must keep them down by any means necessary.

The Dadaist art movement that followed World War One gives a window into a child's world. Children are the only ones left who can carry on the Dadaist work of surprising, shocking, and confounding, because the world is now being run by zombies who have been programmed to acquire money above all else. Without any foreknowledge of the movement, children will recreate Dadaism as long as they have not been mentally immobilized by screens large and small. It's taken me several years to relate to their crazy art, but now, thanks to my experience as Dada himself, I finally get it. Here on Planet Da Dad, we nurture the way of being that encourages Dadaist works to sprout, no matter how maddening they may seem once they have been materialized here at home.

For instance, Girl discovered that it's great fun to hang from the fireplace mantle and swing her feet up into the smoke chamber. After getting her bare soles nice and black, she stomps around on the wood floor, leaving footprints so inky and perfect that they appeared to be drawn by a magic marker. With this technique, she transformed the living room into an eerie space where it seemed that the ghost of child coal miner had wandered, lost and aimless. I clean it all up and in my mindlessness, scolded her, but the experience was simply too compelling to forego. She did it all over again the next day. The day after that, she dialed it up a notch by smearing tiger balm all over herself and the floor, adding a little tactile zing, spicy aroma, and slipperiness to the whole affair. The living room had become a place for contemplating the roles of spontaneity, fire, disorder and direction in our lives. I decided to let it be.

Boy's creative instinct is no less Dadaist, but it takes the form of performance art that unfolds in real time. He puts himself into imaginary battles and fights with every type of human, animal, and alien adversary. All it takes is a stick, and the dance to the death is on. I guess we could call it acting, except that he's a monologist playing all the parts. Battles commence as we walk down the sidewalk, saunter through the woods, or cook dinner in the backyard. He knows every type of sword, rapier, and club that was used throughout the ages, and he's customized the walls and woodwork of our house with his weaponry. Are these kids making art? It depends upon on your aesthetic, not to mention your tolerance, but the very fact that you're asking this question means that it is probably anti-art, ART of the Dadaist school. They alter your landscape, and reconfigure your mindscape. Most works of art by adults exalt the ego. Children teach us that real art exalts the soul of the maker during the making.

Like trickster fairies of Native American or Irish lore, the little people bring down sheer madness on your life, but that anti-rational state of mind suggests something more, something beyond our ready grasp. They offer the antidote to our over-programmed, over-structured, over-commodified world, if only I can tear them away from the TV set. They say amusing and even poetic things, yet they display their real magic by causing you to utter lines such as, "stop waving your pants over your head and put them back on!" Which brings me back to an important question posed earlier: who lives in a pineapple under the sea? The answer, of course, is Sponge Bob, the only contemporary cartoon that brings back the full fury of creative nonsense while somehow also making weird sense. It's a comedy show for grown-ups masquerading as a cartoon for kids. My favorite character is Plankton, who gives voice to the show's writers and sounds just like me. "I command you to stop that!" he barks, "stop that and return to your post! Where's the off button on this thing?" By their hijinx, what kids are really trying to teach us is that the world is not ruled by money, or the conflict between good and evil, but by the synergy of chaos and imagination. They're protean creatures in both realms, capable of invoking either force as readily as their next breath. To them, every strange scrap of trash is just waiting to be reborn as something entirely different in the service of fun or aesthetic transformation. Old mop handles become martial arts weapons, dirty sheets become tents, pruned branches become huts, plastic refuse becomes a sculpture, and rolls of scotch tape hold it all together. It all comes down to making art in the service of fun=god.

Laurel and Hardy are the fools who best reflect the conflict between the worldviews held by adults and children. Oliver is the father figure who's nominally in charge, but his over-confident bluster and impatience are easily manipulated by flattery, especially coming from some femme fatale. Stan is the child, full of imagination, creative magic, and desperate tears. He speaks common sense and sees right through Oliver's specious dreams, but Oliver's vanity and ego prevent him from hearing Stan's wisdom until all his plans and schemes blow-up to disastrous effect. They both live in imaginary worlds, but the adult tries to deny his fairytale dreams while the child admits to them and is thus allowed to perform magic. Like another holy fool, Don Quixote, SAHDs are knights errant on a sacred duty in a profane world. Hence, at times we can sound slightly crazed to those who unquestioningly accept the insanity of modern life, which may or may not explain this chapter to you, depending on whether you've been experienced.

I must be serious for a moment though and give credit to the many adults out there who're working hard to change things. They've come up with creative ideas for a better economic arrangement, like the green economy, the transition economy, and my particular favorite, the sharing economy. But kids over the age of 6 know us well enough to know that we'll make a mess of things no matter how good our intentions. They see all the spoiled, superstitious, ungrateful, and belligerent children out there masquerading as adults all running amok. They know that we overvalue material things, and undervalue everything else. Change will come only when adults realize that they will be marked as failures by doing one of two things: 1) selling junk to kids, or 2) harming the world they live in. Everything else is fair game, so have a blast, but take note that points 1 and 2 represent much bigger nets than one might think at first glance.

On the cover of this week's New Yorker, a woman is pushing a stroller into a playground filled with other parents tending their kids. Closer inspection reveals that all of the parents in the park are men. The phenomenon I've been boring you with is suddenly now everywhere. Once again, I've gone from ten years ahead of a major trend, to being too far behind to capitalize on it. At this point, my prospective publisher will put down this manuscript and send out their form rejection letter, unless they're a self-publishing house, in which case they'll gladly take both your money and mine. No, wait a minute, here's another article about electronic publishing! Maybe I can have it both ways. Yes, I will go on. So bear with me a trifle longer, dear reader, and I promise you'll be rewarded with more pearls of wisdom as soon as they come to me.

Sunday Morning Sleeping-In

Up at 5:00am.

Where's Dada?

Boy cleverly used his first day at school to plan his escape strategy. The stern teacher took him into the hallway as punishment for some infraction, and there he saw his opening. The next morning, he intentionally caused some disturbance upon entering the classroom and the teacher took the bait. She marched him out of the classroom for a time-out, and the moment she turned her back, he bolted for daylight down the longest hallway in the world. The children in one classroom after another caught sight of him sprinting past, and they burst into cheers for the runner who was living out their repressed dreams of flight. He glanced over his shoulder and saw a teacher's aide trying to corral all the other boys who wanted to follow his streak for freedom. Like some tiny Spartacus in the making, the thought of a school-wide insurrection flashed through his mind.

I was in the schoolyard talking with another parent when the door blasted open and Boy dashed out like an escapee from a super-max facility. He ran into my arms saying, "I'm not going back. I'm not going back no matter what you say!" The curtain had closed on a special period in his life—one of freedom and fellowship with me, and he wasn't going to give it up without a fight. "I'm staying with you," he demanded, "I want to be home schooled!" I looked up at the door window, which framed the teacher's face, contorted now in a grim expression of outrage at such rebelliousness. She didn't dare open that door because several other boys had escaped from various classrooms and followed mine in his run for liberty. I later learned that it is supposedly up to the police to handle little fugitives who make it past the school walls. Supermax, indeed.

I was able to calm him down, reassure him that everything would be okay, and slowly coax him back inside. Later in the week, he bolted a second time and came running to me once again. The poor little man hated school, but more than that, he loved being with me. His actions were a gift to our relationship, and I swore to do my best from then on out. For the next several mornings, I got up with him at dawn to do his homework. Then he wanted to go for a jog, which we did. Over time, he bravely accommodated himself to 6 hours in the classroom, every moment of which he described as "dreadful," and akin to "jumping into a tub of hot lava." Who's kidding whom? School sucks. Boy faced a bad situation head on and dealt honestly with his feelings from the get-go. He had reacted the same way when I dropped him off at preschool a few years earlier. He locked onto my leg with all of his strength and cried his heart out. A kind-hearted young teacher had to pry him off and hold him tightly while I escaped for a couple of hours of paying work that seemed essential, at the time.

Perhaps there is an atavistic element to this behavior, since once upon a time, kids' lives depended upon being able to have their father in full view at all times. I think they're born with an instinctual understanding that losing one's father is an existential threat. For hundreds of thousands of years, we provided physical protection in the rawest sense. We were supposed to be there, club and spear at the ready, in case that neighboring cave bear got a taste for human flesh, or if some wandering tribe wanted your tribe's well. Maybe that's also why Boy was so fascinated, from his earliest age, with weapons of every type. Back in those days, boys had to equip themselves for taking down grown men as soon as possible. Television capitalizes on their need to witness blood sport. My kid's fascination peaked with Zombies versus Vampires, which is a battle surprisingly loaded with permutations, reversals, and symbolism. Make no mistake about it, the little people still feel that you're key to their survival. If they cannot see you, they feel unprepared to take on that zombie or wolf or raging mother, so stick around.

Girl shows her need for me just as strongly, though in a feminine way. The first time I spoke with her on the phone, she had only one question, "Dada, where?" Wife once watched Girl wandering from room to room, calling out my name in a sad, hopeful voice. When she finally accepted the fact that I was nowhere in the house, she curled up on the couch and fell asleep, softly whimpering my name, "Dada. Dada. Dada." That was also the first word spoken by both kids. Having people love and want you that much is why people go into politics, show biz, and bartending. It might even be the reason why you end up being a SAHD.

Another paradox to this job is that my kids need all of my encouragement to not need me. I must put myself out of business by replacing myself with their own competence and resourcefulness as soon as possible. I must sink back down into obscurity; a two-hit wonder whose meteoric rise is followed by a slow, self-induced withdrawal from the limelight. But wait a minute. Boy is in 6th grade, but he would still rather spend the day with me than in school with his compatriots. Girl still spills out her heart to me, considers me a great friend, and revels in joining me in whatever I'm doing. That is not dependence. That is enjoyment of each other's company.

Meditations in an Emergency

Most men feel that they have a chance of dealing with any tangible problem. The intangible is another matter altogether, like having your small child vanish without a trace, even if only for a few minutes. Should this ever happens to you, sheer terror will scramble your brain, make your heart slide up into your throat, and if it goes on long enough, your ears will begin ringing like the Bells of St. Mary's. You will use logic and speed and every creative approach, yet ultimately, the utter blankness where there was once a human being is so mystifying that your brain threatens to overload. Within a fraction of a second, you find that you have been dropped into the Twilight Zone where reality cannot really be happening.

I've been through this monstrous experience twice, once for each child, and nothing, not even my own near-death, has gripped me with more dread.

The first time was in Hershey, Pennsylvania, where both kids were born. We managed to avoid going to Hershey Amusement Park during the entire five years we lived there. Then, on our last night in town, we figured it was either now or never. It should have been never. The summer season was over, and the Park stayed open mainly for locals who were allowed to skip the outrageously high admission price and pay by the ride. Boy was rattled that he wasn't tall enough for some of the rides he wanted to endure. We went with another couple who also brought along their young kids, so he had company on the kiddee rides, but some kids are born adventurers, and they will find ways to do what you do not want them to do.

As we ventured deeper into the Park, the adults enjoyed a few moments of conversation, which is all that it took. I looked around and realized that Boy had vanished, and I also suddenly realized that the Park was an enormous maze of dark pathways spread over 120 acres. Ominous shadows ruled the place that moments before had looked just like any other amusement park trying to conserve energy in the post-season. We all split up and began combing the area where we last saw him. With each passing minute, the tension rose exponentially. The strange thing was how I felt such an immediate and total separation between myself and all of the other people in the crowd. One moment I with them, enjoying the rides in the late summer night air, but the next moment I was swallowed up by a black hole. Remember at these times to maintain your link to those other people in that other world, because you will be too frantic to think straight and they're the ones who will find your kid.

We spent an eternity of racing around that sprawling Park, searching every nook and cranny, but to no avail. All the worst scenarios began running through my head when someone caught a glimpse of what looked like a small child in the seat of an adult ride that was heading up its track and getting ready for one of those whirling, dropping, sickening motions for which people pay top dollar. Boy had evaded us and doubled back to go on one of the rides he was too small to take. The depraved teenager at the controls said that he had been letting Boy ride that death machine over and over again because the tiny tike had assured him that it was okay with his parents. I was so relieved that I could not be angry, for there was Boy, happy and victorious in his independence. And there I was, 20 years older in only 10 minutes. Time takes on a different meaning when you lose sight of a child.

I once met a woman who had lived in my old apartment complex in lower Manhattan, until a startling experience propelled her out of the city 20 years earlier. She was pushing her baby stroller along First Avenue one morning when she stopped to buy a newspaper. She turned to pay the vender, turned back toward her stroller, and found a strange woman deftly lifting her baby out of it. The shock of interrupting a kidnapping in progress left her speechless. The child-snatcher piped up first, "oh, is this *your* baby?" Yes, thanks, and I'll take him back now. That horror was enough to launch her family 200 miles out to the Pennsylvania countryside, whence she never returned.

My second brush with disappearance also happened under the cover of darkness, and once again, my child around 3 years old. This time it was Girl, who was having a bedtime tantrum. I placed her wiggling body down in her bed with some authority and told her not to get out. She responded by following me to the door and slamming it shut as I left. Sometimes, no, oftentimes you will find that you don't have the energy to engage in kid battles with the composure of a lion tamer. In this case, I was glad just to get out of there and just let her stew in her room awhile. An hour later, I went in to make sure that she was covered up, but the bedroom was empty. She wasn't in the bathroom, either. Nor was she in Boy's room, nor hiding under his covers, nor anywhere upstairs. I began calling out her name as though she were a misbehaving golden retriever. Girl! Girl? Since this was New Jersey, it was hard to not immediately think, Lindbergh baby. I had to banish that thought, or at least shelve it, so that I could launch into a systematic search through every room in the house. Check all the windows. Closets. Drawers and cupboards. Attic. Basement. Outside. No luck. Okay, stay calm, and do it all over again with greater care and diligence. The result was the same. Nothing. By the time we were repeating the cycle a third time, both Wife and I are screaming for GIRL! Once again, we had fallen down the rabbit hole. That raging toddler had just up and disappeared. It was freaky.

Emergencies of this import have the curious power of being able to stop time. You become completely and utterly stuck in the present where every second counts, since Girl could be suffocating or choking to death somewhere on our property, or worse. Yet, we were in that different dimension where logic gets exhausted. The past and the future disappeared as we focused on performing the trick of finding Girl. We searched everywhere, for about 20 minutes, and then called the cops. They came complete with a missing person's detective, and began searching meticulously as we'd done three, or some infinite number of times already. When the call came that "we found her!" I nearly fell to my knees. The future came raging back into view.

Girl had crawled up two shelves inside a narrow linen closet, closed the door, burrowed herself to the back wall behind stacks of sheets, and fallen fast asleep. All the cops came to take a look at the instructive sight. She never even woke up when we placed her back into her bed.

Having a child vanish is the most visceral fear imaginable. The surge of adrenaline I had endured in the face of that apparent hopelessness had aged me yet another 20 years. So my true age, as in a dog's life, is now somewhere around 80. I must also have PTSD, for there have been many other times when I've been in that state of growing terror, only to be told by someone to simply turn around and look down, when, presto! My kid would magically appear. May all parents of lost kids find them just as easily.

The disappearance of a single child in New York changed the way that children in America lead their lives. The story of 6 year-old Eton Patz and the search conducted by his bereft parents captivated the nation 34 years ago, and police are still searching for him today. Right now, they're hammering open some basement in Soho, but the only thing entombed there is the carefree way that kids enjoyed life when I was growing up. The overwhelming media attention given to the Patz case planted a viral fear deep into the heart of every parent, a fear that has ruined the social ecosystems of kids' neighborhoods. In the days before that case, we were given bikes instead of babysitters, and expected to use them to go find something to do. We'd be free to explore, and when we'd worn ourselves out, or when the sun began to set or our stomachs began to growl, we'd head home.

Nowadays, playdates are arranged a week in advance. Bikes and fields have been traded for basements and nannies, which are not necessarily safer and do nothing to develop a child's decision-making ability. After years of playing videogames in dank basements, some kids just go out and shoot people in large numbers. Others fail to learn the basics of peer interactions because they're given the run of the house by clueless babysitters. One 5 year-old in our neighborhood turned out to be an ardent French kisser who practiced his delicious art in the darkness of the family basement with multiple partners. It wasn't until his entire preschool class began to show oral herpes sores that the truth came out about his amorous adventures. Independent bike riding and walking among kids has decreased drastically, all replaced by idiotic smart phones, whereby kids summon their chauffeurs. In turn, the number of cars on the road has increased wildly, and with them, the real and primary danger to children: the car, especially curb-hopping SUVs, means that kids are no longer safe even up on the sidewalk. Expensive mini-trucks are flying all over the place, often flipping over in their drivers' mindless rush to nowhere. We should all wonder whether taking away our kids' freedom of movement and association means that are we're raising a generation of citizens acclimated to giving away their independence whenever it seems safer to do so.

The Wild Kingdom

To man and woman each were given their place, and they found it was good. Girls found that it was good to create and cooperate. Boys found that it was good to destroy and compete. Their atavistic behavior manifests the essential Hindu belief that the universe goes through cycles of creation and destruction. Women are always making things, (such as human beings, for example), and men are always destroying things (likewise). In my house, Girl enjoys taking hours to create miniature kingdoms, which Boy will gleefully destroy in seconds. This script gets replayed endlessly as the two jarringly different worldviews clash in the living room. I assure you that it is nature, not nurture, and so yelling and whatever punishments I can think up to stop the destruction are futile. When confronted with Shiva, the great destroyer, all I can do is give equal worship to Krishna, the great creator, and hope some cosmic symmetry will teeter into balance in my house.

The innate differences between boys and girls are reflected in the polar opposite categories of toys that they enjoy. Our house is an armory of weapons that fire water, gel pellets, foam bullets, and all manner of harmless missiles. War technology from every century finds representation in the array of swords and shields and catapults and guns lying about the place. Then there are the art-making materials, the dolls that can be variously dressed, the jewelry making sets, the custom nail polish mixing kit, and the games that engage girls in creative, non-competitive interplay. We did not foist these items upon them. They were bought only after much pleading at garage sales, and neither child shows any interest in the category of toys possessed by the other. The differences are striking even when there are no toys around and they're left to their own imaginations.

On our walk through the woods this morning, the three of us were off the pavement only a few minutes before boy and girl fell into their respective roles. Boy found a Y shaped branch that he wanted to make into a slingshot for hunting deer, and he went off to collect nice round stones to use as projectiles. Girl sat in the leaves and started "sowing" very intently, threading a tiny twig thru the delicate holes in a dead oak leaf. When I tried to move things along and it dropped to the ground, she cried, "My sowing! My sowing!" I couldn't help but let her sow awhile longer, and reassure her that we'd give her lots of sowing one day. Boy was equally heartbroken when he dropped a couple of his round rocks into the leaves and couldn't find them. These two kids, only 4 and 2 years old, fell straightaway into tasks they found perfectly normal and fully absorbing.

The sweep of womankind and mankind are on display each day that one gets to watch a young girl and a young boy in the process of growing up. Girl loves holidays, and must make sure that the house is decorated appropriately, and various rituals observed with care. Boy has no idea when they're coming, nor does he care to know, with the sole exception of Christmas, because it might bring him a new weapon of imaginary mass destruction. Girl makes lists in preparation for the holidays: people to invite, games to play, foods to make. Boy has never thought of making a list. Girl forces me to take her to church, but no one can drag Boy in there. This all makes it clear, once again, that women have built civilization. Unfortunately, they must therefore also accept more of the blame for it. Though job discrimination might still be rampant, we do not live in some simple patriarchal arrangement.

If natural inclinations are apparently hard-wired by gender, how did I end up in a "woman's job?" There are historical stories of women taking on men's jobs, such as Joan of Arc, Hilary Clinton, and the Amazons, but never do you read about men taking on women's jobs. SAHDs must therefore represent a strange and wonderful experiment to bridge the chasm between life-giving and life-taking. As such, our success or failure will determine the fate of the planet. How about that for re-inflating the deflated ego of the male childcare giver? In truth, the gender roles might hold because I cannot really claim to be a baby wrestler--I didn't actually take on the job until they were toddlers, at which point, they were very different animals. For those who are having any anxieties regarding the mash-up of "roles," perhaps thinking of this job as animal husbandry will keep it squarely within the masculine sphere and out of the way of any concerns over gender-bending. After all, I am growing a crop of people here.

You see, there's the feeding (first bottles, then oats, then mish-mashed slop), the pasturing (carpets, then lawns, then playgrounds, then playing fields), the herding (corralling, guiding, walking, then driving), the bathing (increasingly larger tubs, then hosing down), the manure removal (self-explanatory), and last but not least, the breeding (sex talks, boyfriend vetting, rejection of poor mates). I'm raising really smart animals for the specific purpose of improving upon and replacing me. Hence, I am no threat to the immutable gender roles, which remain intact despite appearances and mislabeling.

There do seem to be marked differences, however, in ways in which men and women run households with children. The homes of my male compatriots in this struggle all seem to have the same spirit of combined playfulness and practicality that marks them as essentially "father." This style exists by accident and not by design, though a certain precarious equilibrium can be detected upon closer investigation. In the big playpen that I call home, we try to strike a karmic balance between toys for destruction and toys for creation. For every sword that arrives, there must be a new paint set; for every machine gun, a block of sculpting clay; for every battle axe, a building set; and so on. As I pointed out at the beginning of this section, sometimes these elements clash, to the glee of the destroyer and sorrow of the creator. But culture is being made and destroyed, just as it has been throughout human history, right here at home on a daily basis. This dynamic process unfolds as long as there are no screens spewing out their compelling nonsense to distract the creators and destroyers from pursuing their natural inclinations.

One thing you will notice, when men rule the household, is that intentional destruction is tolerated a bit more, perhaps in recognition of its place as the other key force in the universe. The busted shit is allowed to remain on display for a time, almost like an avant garde art installation, after which it disappears when no one is looking, making way for the cycle to continue unabated. At the same time, deeper inspection reveals a capriciousness in our homes, too. A man on the job might have a basement ready to engage the kids in any number of outdoor activities, but that house would also be less prepared for the essentials of life. The same house ruled by a woman might not have sleds, tennis racquets, bats, cleats, ice skates, bikes, helmets, skis, and balls of every type, but it would have plenty of food, drink, and medicines. Once again, it is clearly women who kept us all going throughout the ages that included the Bubonic Plague, the Wisconsin Glacier, volcanic eruptions, and various wars of extermination. If it had been up to us men, we would have had one big party, and then let the human race go extinct. It could be that we are in fact trying to do just that, but it's unfolding in slow motion due to the countervailing influence of the female culture makers and healers. My house is a good example, where there is enough beer for Armageddon, yet never enough toilet paper.

Boy shows strong adherence to the male tendency towards the love of destruction, so when he wanted a computer, we had him build one. He needed a desk on which to put it, so we built one of those with him, too. They're the direct result of his own ingenuity, patience, and ability to cooperate with another person on a complex task. Many items around the house that magically appeared in exchange for money were the victims of his abuse, but neither the computer nor the desk have been harmed in any way. The main lesson I hope he learned is that idolatry must not be wasted on money, but should be reserved for more deserving things, like season one of the original Star Trek.

Dance Dance Revolution

Dance does not usually spring to mind first when ranking the subversive power of various art forms. Yet today, it provoked such a dangerous threat that the school principal summoned me into his office for an emergency intervention. It seemed that Boy had started an insurrection by dancing during his first grade music class. Upon observing him cutting loose, his fellow inmates began to hear the music within themselves, too, and in short order the entire class was dancing their tensions away. I don't know if a rhumba line was formed, or whether the artistry was limited to individual free-form expression, but I came to understand that the music had penetrated their seven year-old souls, wherein it had found full and free outlet through their rhythmic movements. At this point, one would think that the teacher would recognize that her musical appreciation class was succeeding beyond her wildest expectation. But I could see from the principal's pained expression that this was not so. On the contrary, the prim young teacher had thrown herself into a tilted attempt to control the animal spirits that she felt were threatening to overtake her classroom, and by extension, her very soul.

"Stop! Everyone please STOP!" she commanded them, but the music was all they heard. The sight of her students reinventing post-modernism right before her eyes had become too disorienting. In desperation, she went after the lead shaman, Boy, and attempted to exorcise the musical spirits from him. When that effort failed, she found herself hopelessly overcome by the whole bacchanalian scene, and she fled the room in horror. Once safely outside the classroom, she leaned against the wall, and attempted to regain her composure by performing deep breathing exercises. Art had been radically democratized, and as such, it was perceived as a major security threat to the authorities. They clamped down hard by calling in reinforcements to quell the rebellious dancing. Further corrective measures would be necessary to right this heinous wrong. Hence I found myself face to face with the face of school order and propriety.

The principal showed me a letter he wrote condemning the "deplorable behavior." He had clearly dug deep into the thesaurus to come up with that many condemning words, which he had then packed into four terse paragraphs that sounded like he was writing about a terrorist act. Without once mentioning the word dancing, he described the children's behavior as without precedent, one that would lead to excommunication should it ever be repeated. The dance revolution launched by 7 year-olds shows why some religions outlaw dancing altogether: anyone can do it, well, almost anyone. Dancers feel freer during the act, and if performed with proper abandon, they will afterwards feel less willing to accept all the various straightjackets our culture tries to impose. Best to stop that trend in early childhood, lest we revert back to a simpler time before people gave up control over their lives to screens and corporations and governments and banks and schools and religions.

The principal said, "that letter will go into his permanent file." Yikes. He's getting life for it. Must have been quite a performance. Sorry I missed it. Bravo!

The Year of Plumbing Dangerously

"Hey Dad, it's raining in the dining room!" This strangely poetic line sent me dashing over to find that rain was indeed falling from the ceiling, and a curtain of water was descending down the walls. It looked as though an indoor waterfall had been installed that embraced you on all sides, which would be fun if you hadn't just restored those walls and it wasn't your house. But of course, you did, and it is, so you must stop dinner once again and scramble around like mad until you find buckets for collection, the source of the water, and the number of the plumber. By that time, the kids and the dog will have taken the opportunity of having water covering the dining room floor to slide from one end to the other, crashing into furniture along the way. The American dream of homeownership will be in full flower, and you will be thankful for those two mortgages you are carrying that allow you to witness such a gleeful scene.

If you're a SAHD who is cursed with the ability to swing a hammer, you will find yourself renovating your home while also trying to take care of kids who're breathing asbestos, eating lead paint chips, and playing with box cutters all the while. In my case, I bought an old house that was in such bad shape that a ceiling caved in when the home inspector walked on the roof above it. Unfortunately, the octogenarian owner was sitting under the falling plaster at the time, thus increasing his motivation to sell the house, even as I was becoming less inclined to buy it. We eventually found a point at which his desperation to get out met my trepidation to get in, and we became the proud owners of a 1933 colonial revival that needed everything. In order to afford the cost of making it a safe place to live, never mind restoring or updating it, I would have to do most of the work myself. Do not try this at home, especially not while you're supposed to be watching the kids. On the other hand, if you ignore my advice and proceed to restore an old house, your kids will see you actually transforming the material world around them, and hopefully for the better. The empowering, positive effects that has had on my kids seems to have offset the negative effects of my yelling at them to stop chewing on that epoxy. I shall leave it up to you to strike your own balance.

If you must follow in my footsteps, be prepared to hear a call for help that will arrive, without fail, while you are cooking dinner on the stove. "Dad! The toilet is overflowing again. But really bad this time!" Remember to turn off the fire before racing to dive into the brown water that's pooling over the bathroom floor and threatening to spill into the adjacent room. Water likes to surprise people. Just wait till you see what it's got up it's sleeve for sometime around mid-century along all the coasts. Anyway, when you buy an old house, you're actually buying an ancient network of pipes that are out of sight and out of mind, until they burst in sets of threes. Sometimes, they pop on the top floor and fill your house like a giant aquarium. Other times, they get clogged outside and you must domicile a group of teamsters until such time as they are satisfied that you have no money left and no credit line untapped. Usually, all of these fates will befall you within a single 12 month period, because pipes in different places are inclined to fail all at once, as though the entire network were some kind of watery time bomb. You can get insurance against this eventuality, but you will become tired of making the monthly payments, and cancel it. But your pipes are smart than you, and they will wait until the very moment that you have signed the cancelation notice to send out the signal to attack. Consider yourself forewarned.

Burnin' Down the House!

Children manifest their emotions in the most direct ways available to them. Like today, when I picked Girl up from school, and we headed for a happy rendezvous with matza ball soup and an egg white omelet. All went swimmingly until the ride home, when she realized that I had committed the mortal sin of skipping the toy store. I was ordered me to return to the store post haste, and furthermore, that I apologize for blatantly disregarding her toy envy. The swoop into our driveway finalized the answer I had been giving her the whole way home. Her rebuttal was equally swift and definitive: an epic nuclear tantrum that nearly cost us everything we own.

In our house, crying is perfectly acceptable. They can wail all they want to—in their rooms. In keeping with this wise stricture, I removed her into the house and told her to go up to her room to cry it out. She complied without further escalating hostilities, which seemed very odd, but I was so grateful to be relieved of the sonic assault that I gave it little further thought. After the ringing in my ears subsided, I grew suspicious of the quiet, and followed a strong feeling that I should go to check on her. Never, ever ignore that little parental voice in your head. You are dumb and it is smart. Always listen to and obey your inner father. It's probably the only reason that our species is still capering about the place.

I bounded up to her room, opened the door and found her sitting on the floor. "There!" she said proudly, thinking that she had set up a nice breezy fan, when in fact she had placed a powerful electric space heater upside down and on full blast, so that heat was blazing straight down against the red oak floor. If I had arrived 30 seconds later, the entire room would have burst into flames. The poor little wronged girl, sent to her room in tears and tantrums, had found a way to express her red-hot anger. In an impressive show of stealth, she had entered my office, unplugged the heater, sequestered it up the stairs, plugged it back in and turned it on, all without being seen. The whole mission was pretty impressive for a 4 year-old to conceive and execute. The art of destruction is not her milieu, and her first work might have been accidental, but it would have also been monumental.

At least once in their lives, most kids will attempt to torch your big-shot, grown up world. If you're lucky, they'll succeed in doing so, but slowly, over the course of several years, so that you barely perceive the change occurring, and not all at once.

Let's Roll

Getting out of the door will usually take almost an hour, and many months off your life. Do not expect appreciation for your foreshortened lifespan. In fact, why bother leaving home at all? Better to stay a shut-in. Claim agoraphobia and be done with it. Or just let them amble out of the door naked and barefoot, preferably in the snow, until they figure out that clothes and footwear are not your idea. The way of the hard-earned lesson might be preferable to my drill sergeant routine, which is generally ineffectual anyway, but does seem to relieve some of my stress. Better to let it out than keep it bottled up, I say. Or maybe just start the day with a nice glass of Pinot Noir and let all the rest roll off your shoulders. I've never done that, but it sure sounds like a good recommendation to you.

Before kids, it used to take me 5 seconds to prepare to leave the house. Just grab the keys and go. Now, the struggle starts with socks, which have become instruments of torture. Kids figure that Einstein didn't wear them, so why should they? Who are you to squash a budding genius? Mr. Nasty, that's who, and on the socks must go. Next there are the shoes, which are always lost. Wait a minute, I almost forgot about the clothes. Here, put on your pants. Such a rude suggestion is certainly a cryable offence. Boy, go downstairs and see if her shoes are down there. "Dad, stay right there at the top of the stairs where I can see you," he says, still scared of the basement. Girl wants to follow him. My response in the negative unleashes a manic squirming fit. Boy hollers that they're not down there. A whole house search proves fruitless. Must use other shoes regardless of fit. "They're too tight!" But on they must go. More bleating cries. Uh-oh, forgot Boy's lunch. "I have to go pee-pee," Girl says. Okay, but we're outside and I'll be damned if I'm going to allow the momentum to backslide, so I lift her up and we're done. Okay. Bathing suit. Check. Towel. Check. Keys. Check. Dog barking furiously outside. Must corral him. Not easy as he is faster than any NFL wide receiver. Oops. No wallet. Who cares? The TV flicks on upstairs. One of them snuck back inside for a screen peek. Rage at that fact! First yell of the day to "turn if off!" Then, "Dad, I have to go poo-poo." Everybody back upstairs for that one. She must work through it slowly, but to no avail. Back downstairs to the car, crying the whole way—her, not me. Wow! We're outside! Girl insists on buckling the seat belt herself. Interminable wait. Meanwhile, Boy is leaning forward to fiddle with dashboard controls, and he smashes the blinker arm down, where it hangs by its wire. $300 gone. More crying. I notice the door to the house is open and Dog is back outside again and I don't care. I'm off, now, or never will be.

Doctors, Dentists, Barbers, and Blog-based Business Promoters

What was the world like before experts existed? For one thing, there was more time, and much more money. People cut hair themselves. Minor illnesses, cuts and bruises were treated at home. Don't get me wrong, I'm glad health care professionals exist for those times when we really need them, but people seem to have lost the ability to handle even the simplest of things at home anymore.

Let's start with pediatricians, those underpaid, overworked guardians of child health. Taking your kid on a routine "well baby" checkup means you'll arrive with a well baby but return with a sick one. The germs being shared in the waiting rooms are vicious and layered thick in the carpets and smeared on the toys. Other kids toddle around those places with runny noses, sneezing lice out of their hair, and drooling on your kid. Let me be clear: I admire pediatricians. They've chosen to forgo making real money because they want to work with kids. They're relatively meager salary is another reflection of the value we place on children. The way we pay teachers is another.

Dentists are an interesting case because they give your kid gas, which kids love so much that they'll stop brushing their teeth just to get cavities and a nice gas trip to cartoon land. It's a kick to see a kid smiling away while getting her teeth drilled. In the old day, we'd be slamming doors attached by strings to rotten teeth, which would scare the kids straight into brushing their teeth on their own, hence reducing but not eliminating the need for a dentist, who seem to exist in a happy symbiotic relationship with barbers. Barbers give kids lollipops as a reward for sitting still for 5 minutes in the chair, which in turn sends them to the dentist, who extracts more money from their parents while complimenting the kids on their neat haircuts, starting the cycle anew.

With self-reliance going by the wayside, and in the scramble to make ends meet, hucksters have descended upon harried parents like vultures on road kill. Did you know that by spending just a few hours a day on the computer, you too can make $5400 a month? It's brilliant how blog-based business promoters came up with that number, which represents the realistic pre-tax bottom line needed to keep a family of 4 respectably housed, fed, and shod in America today. And all you have to do is buy their package, and the internet money machine will do the rest! Poor besieged parents with minds addled and jangled by the wee people will grasp at anything that promises relief. They're become even easier marks for advertisers than their children.

The Things They Carried

You'll be amazed at the things you dig out of your pockets with absolutely no recollection of how they got in there. There will be small chokeables of all description, well-chewed rubber bands, tiny filthy socks, ray guns, slimy pennies, sticky bits of food packaging, indecipherable love notes written in hieroglyphics of their own invention, and that roll of Menthos they pilfered by slipping it into your pocket surreptitiously on the grocery check-out line. You'll be in real trouble if you ever dare to wear cargo pants. It will be equally shocking to find what you do not have in there, such as your keys, wallet, cell phone, and shopping list. Sometimes they will be in there, but hopelessly lost in the debris. Other times these important items will have simply disappeared altogether. That is another part of the magic of childhood.

You can just try carrying everything, including your kids, around in a backpack, at least until they reach the age of puberty. I once carried Boy, who was a 20 month-old toddler at the time, in a backpack all the way down the Big Arsenic Spring trail in the Wild Rivers area of the Rio Grande Canyon. Sweeping vistas and thousand-foot drop offs greet you along the way to the bottom, where the river is a shallow, pristine blue stream tumbling over smooth rocks, and swirling into small bays where watercress grows in abundance. I took off his shoes and let him wade into the cold shallows. He badly wanted to plunge into the deep center-stream, but this lifeguard was off-duty, so we went to investigate some pictographs on a gathering of red boulders nearby. He delighted in wandering around that ancient art gallery, and was probably the youngest human to touch those rock carvings in a thousand years. Somehow, the scene made perfect sense. So get used to carrying them and their stuff wherever you want to go. Otherwise, you will become a pitiful shut-in, and they will hate you even more.

Our Mothers

Left alone, houses and everything in them become giant petrie dishes for all sorts of demonic creatures whose job it is to sweep people into the next world with extreme prejudice. Mold colonizes walls and lungs; bacteria of startling variety explode around toilets and leap onto unsuspecting frequenters; viruses settle comfortably into rugs until some mammal stirs them up, whence they find new quarters in eyes, noses, and gastro-intestinal tracts. Flesh eating bacteria, tuberculosis, e-coli, salmonella, and a host of other microscopic terrorists are lying in wait for the unsuspecting. Where does it all lead? To the doctor's office, whose waiting room constitutes the singular meeting place wherein all these unfriendlies gather to romp unopposed.

My mother, and my guess is, most women know these facts deep in their bones, below the level where they can be easily communicated, because they have lost billions of children to these home invaders over the centuries, more than in all the wars dreamed up by men. Whether consciously or unconsciously, mothers will take whatever means necessary to vanquish these microscopic terrorists before they have the chance to strike down the people they love.

Now, when a man takes over the house, he has none of the ingrained wisdom brought about by this sad fact. He must learn the hard way to keep house, that is, unless he was housebroken by a mother who forced him to help her clean. Growing up in my house meant sacrificing a good chunk of every Saturday morning to my mother's cleaning regime that seemed to reflect an evil deeply rooted in her soul which could find expiation only through the penance of cleaning house. It has taken me nearly half a century to begin to see the atavistic wisdom of her ways. It was not a personal vendetta against me after all. She had inherited from her maternal line a hatred for invisible things that might steal her children away from her. It was an ancient imperative as strong as the will to live, and I was no match for it.

A SAHD without such an upbringing will hopefully experience a brush with reality strong enough to turn the light on in his brain, but not strong enough to turn it off in one of his children. He will come to understand the strategic and tactical nature of this special warfare, and the need to enlist foot soldiers from within his own ranks. He will overcome his fear of becoming his own mother when he assumes the mantle as the most deadly agent in this scorched earth encounter. In other words, he will get a housecleaner from Latin America and supply her with non-toxic cleaning agents. Hygiene is still taken seriously down there, where death from little invisibles is remains a common occurrence. You must also supervise your in-house crew in the performance of daily chores, but understand that you are not up to the full job, which must be handed over to someone who will come in once and awhile to enforce some bottom standard below which your house must not be allowed to fall.

However, as an enlightened male housekeeper, you must also come to understand the difference between clean dirt and dirty dirt. Nothing builds a strong immune system like having a dirty older brother and a big hairy dog in the house. They ensure adequate exposure to the panoply of relatively harmless germs and bacteria that one confronts on any given day, so there will be no surprises when your children present their immune systems to the wider world. On the other hand, people used to have no idea how polio was transmitted, which suggests that there is a balance to be maintained when putting this knowledge into practice.

Our Fathers

One might be inclined to think that men who take care of their kids are overcompensating for being the victims of absent or bad fathers. On the contrary, all the SAHDs I know had very good fathers. Mine has always supported my decision to take care of the kids--there wasn't even any need to discuss it. He has the multiple purple hearts and other medals from being in the drama that we call, with no irony, the European Theater during World War II. Warriors understand the brevity of life, and so the decision to spend each day with one's family makes perfect sense to them. Guys who went through these types of experiences know that work is something good to do, as opposed to a job, which was what their nutso superior officers had and lorded over them. These days, you hear politicians talking about jobs all the time, about how everyone needs them, and how they will deliver jobs unto them if they only vote the right way. But the politicians are wrong. People want meaningful work—which is something far above the level of just having a job. SAHDs and MAHDs have work. People in Congress have jobs.

Any honest search for the reason to why more than half of the women raising children in America today are doing so without a man in the house must consider the role of do-gooders bent on protecting children from their fathers. We can be tough, yes, and stupid too, but these are separate and different and not always mixed together. The typical father figure featured in movies and on TV today is a hitmen at best, or a drunken violent predator at worst. We must protect children from these beastly men! Should we also vilify mothers and remove them from family life because one kills her kids every few days in the U.S.? Of course not, but the only real question is whether the media can make money sensationalizing mommy murderers. So here we are, a nation mostly without fathers, just when fathers are needed more than ever. How much of the degradation of our mass culture can be blamed on fatherless grown-ups, and how much worse will it get, given the trend? It is time for Dads to buck that trend and show back up at home, even if it means unplugging the wireless router that now distributes the propaganda to every room in the house.

Even a quick look at the U.S. president in recent history shows that behind their disastrous ambition you'll find serious father issues. Obama's dad was absent, then dead. GW Bush tried so hard to one-up his dad that he took to pyromania and torched whole countries. Clinton had a violent and abusive step-father. GHW Bush's father was a banker for the Nazis before WWII. Reagan's dad was a dissolute bar owner, and so on. Perhaps these driven men are propelled by a deep need for the attention and acceptance that they didn't get from their fathers. They all received passable mothering, so the problems can't be pinned there. Would the world be a better place if they'd had caring fathers? How about if they even had fathers who were present at all in their lives?

A halfway decent father knows how to add value to being a man on the job. First off, they do not raise their kids to become wimps. If a kid stubs his toe and his father leaps to his rescue, you know how that kid will turn out. If you see a father holding a water bottle in one hand and snacks in the other while staggering along behind his kids just in case they have the slightest thirst or urge to stuff their mouths, you know how they'll turn out. But the kind of toughness you need to imbue is the opposite of the kind that could turn a kid into a bully. It's the kind that has nothing to prove to anyone, except perhaps to themselves. They're the kind who eat all sorts of strange foods when offered, who like nothing better than to try something difficult that they've never tried before, and who aren't afraid of kids different from themselves. We can raise kids who can pick themselves up and dust themselves off, kids who are confident, but not over-confident in that annoying way some kids take up when allowed to marinate in superhero nonsense. The girls we raise will not be afraid to stay at home and care for children regardless of whether their peers jeer, or conversely, to go out and lead a nation. They will be able to fix things, handle a snow shovel, find their way in the woods, and execute a judo throw. They will choose their mates not according to fashion or illusion, but on their ability to handle difficult situations.

I'm proud to say that my kids are honest ass-kickers, and the ass they kick is usually mine. Right now, I'm sitting here at home where we've had no power, heat or phone for two weeks courtesy of Hurricane Sandy. It's snowing pretty hard outside as another storm approaches. My kids have never had more fun.

Joseph Heller, the author of *Catch-22* made a fortune writing about adults who acted like children, but ironically, he couldn't stand children acting like children. "I don't do kids," he said, refusing to take part in raising them. His daughter ended up hating him so much that she won't even read his most famous book. The lesson from old Joe is that if you don't do kids, your kids will do you, and perhaps, much, much worse.

A Modest Proposal

An American man is twice as likely to be in jail or on probation than taking care of a child at home. We'd rather be locked up than take on the daunting scope of work called child-raising, a scope of work that is made all the more difficult to perform because it is not even considered to be a job—you are not "working" when you're doing it. Before I took it on, I too thought that the work of raising children was like a hobby, something you did in your spare time, such as keeping an aquarium in your living room. The fact that the sea monkeys I would be raising are in charge of the future was unfathomable. Child-raisers, those befuddled masters of little people, are in fact in charge of the future, yet they get no pay and no respect whatsoever. Then we complain about crime, drugs, and deranged young adults shooting or blowing up scores of their fellow citizens. Under the current arrangement, the prison business will continue to have new or returning customers for generations to come until we resolve the central paradox of this book, and perhaps of our culture itself: there is no future in child-raising, except the future itself.

A recent study calculated the services rendered by a parent caring for a child amounts to a minimum of $113,000 a year. That's quite a bargain when you consider that we pay ten times that amount to keep just one soldier in a war zone for just one year. The fact that we are not even technically at war shows how much easier it is to get the public to spend money killing people than keeping children alive, mentally stable, and on track toward becoming responsible adults. What might happen if men decided to try raising their children instead of funneling their energies into war, weapons development, corporate empire building, criminal enterprises, and presidential politics, to say nothing of space travel, automobile design, and the selling of it all to a benumbed public? Let's put aside the fact that most men, as they are currently programmed, wouldn't last a month on the childcare circuit. The first thing that the typical man engaging the job would discover is that all other career pursuits are actually quite easy games by comparison, with winners and losers and strategies, and it's all basically fun. Men who become SAHDs would wake-up to the daunting reality that they're running an ultra-marathon that will grind on for over a decade and a half. The attrition rate would be high, but a certain number

183

would hold up under the strain, thanks in part to the salary they receive. The revolution would have begun.

All the energy that used to be squandered on mindlessly building up and then destroying things would start pouring into helping children to thrive. It would transform civilization to a degree matched only by the taming of fire. After a few years handling the job, men would begin systematically eliminating dangers that might wipe out their efforts. The air, water, and food would have to be cleaned-up and stringently protected. If the implications of that aren't mind-boggling enough, consider that roadways would have to be made safe, public spending would have to revolve around education in all its forms, and glorifications of violence and war would have to be revealed as the stratagem for selling more of the same. Meanwhile, pediatricians, teachers, childcare givers, and organic farmers would become the most highly valued and compensated members of society. Forget green economies, socialism, corporate fascism, benevolent dictatorships, new age cohousing villages, tea baggers, or occupy wall streeters, to name a few. Just put men in charge of the children and there just might be a future for our species, after all.

I admit that I'm taking the easy way out, yet again, by turning this childcare job into a profession, thereby slipping back into my old comfortable groove as a 'productive' career person. But

I've found a career that suits my clothes, which have been reduced to t-shirts and sweat pants that will be wiped by mouths and noses all day. I give orders to minions who ignore them. I dispel nightmares from little minds, and try to explain the impossible mess that adults have made of the world. I persevere because childcare is the process of growing your own replacements with the hope that they'll become better models. Meanwhile, mass culture is bent on reversing the trend. Gangstas are shown as cool, women as sex objects, stories as excuses for gory fighting, and music as a way to sell the whole package. The only way to counteract this putrid tidal wave is for a parent to become a countervailing cultural force unto him/herself. Good luck with that, but you should be paid to try.

Instead, the trend is quickly moving away from supporting children. The New York Times recently reported that the wage gap between men and women is closing fast. Of course, they made it sound like a very positive development, but what's really happening is not that women are catching up to men, but that everyone is sinking downward, with the gap closing only because men's incomes are dropping faster than women's incomes. Stooges that we are, men are winning the race to the bottom. I have a friend who considers the mass migration of women into the workplace to favor only the super rich, because they're the only ones who benefit from increasing competition in the labor force and the resulting downward pressure on wages.

185

Despite having the best PR people that money can buy, I don't believe that the very wealthy are smart enough to engineer such a massive social trend. They're simply the happy, doltish beneficiaries of a system that now requires two incomes to support a family. Neither parent can afford to stay home and raise their kids anymore. Then we fret over adult children who still live at home because there wasn't a real grown-up present to guide them through the maze of how to live independently with their dignity. The most recent Census put it all in simple terms: there are more Americans living in poverty now than at any time since record-keeping began.

For argument's sake, let's accept my friend's theory for a moment, however paranoid it may be, that the movement of women into the job market is a conspiracy of the capital-owning class. The whole thing would backfire on them if men countered by moving into family care in mass numbers. Woman's salaries would skyrocket due to the sudden contraction of available labor. Once again, a family might be able to subsist on one income, and there would be a parent available to raise the children. In this scenario, the ownership class would quickly and cheaply silence my ilk and stamp out the revolution by shaming men back into their place. How easy would it be to keep us SAHD fools in check? Answer: very, by impugning our manhood's. Call us ninnies, as did a consistently dopey author of a Times column titled "Men are the New Women." We're still too insecure to stand such words, and we will rush back to wage slavedom, unless we find the strength to embrace our inner fools, which our children are happy to help us do. That's our secret weapon, but you must give up any shred of hubris when you go on this job, otherwise you will be shamed out of doing it.

Putting men in charge of the kids at this point in history is a great idea but it threatens the status quo that is the foundation of all the other status quos. So, ignore all of the foregoing. Continue devaluing children and childcare work, dominating women, exploiting the poor, and despoiling the planet. Put zero value on the job of childcare done by parents, and also zero value on the environmental processes that allow the continuance of life on Earth. The air, water, soil, forests, and seas are all free for the taking by those who would destroy them for immediate profit. Our children and our home planet receive the same treatment. Ironically, the real value in each case is beyond any measure. We therefore consider the infinite to be equal to zero, and we give them no price at all. Exploitation ensues readily.

PS: in case you think I've gone completely soft on defense, consider whether it would be a wise move to invade a country of people raised by men like me, whose kids have walked to school virtually everyday regardless of whatever extreme weather they faced, who before the age of 10 could handle tools, execute single leg take-downs, build a computer, and run, swim, and climb like Navy Seals. My plan is hardly a recipe for a weaker nation, but it might provide a cure for the military-financial complex.

Tears, Inconvenience, God, and Poetry

The constant cycle of fighting, crying, blaming, and rending of garments, followed by hugging and making up, might remind you of a bad relationship you've had with another consenting adult. However, I'm talking here about the whirlwind of children's emotions that are always blowing at full blast in your face day and night, especially if you have a vocal girl in your orbit. Either you learn the martial art of deflecting these rampaging passions, or they will knock you out cold. All of those how-to books don't work on this particular pickle either, because child-raising is actually an art form that can't really be taught. You have to feel your way into it. Maybe that's why most women are better at it than most men. They're in better touch with their feelings, and hence better able to surf the emotional tidal waves generated daily by kids.

On the other hand, most men spend their formative years learning to ignore their feelings. Showing anything other than unmitigated glee will label you a wuss. By the time we're called upon to become child caretakers, we have no idea where emotions come from or how they could blow up so dramatically. The one thing we do clearly feel is ambushed by the intensity of our kids' emotions. At least it's a start. From there, you can begin to explore your other feelings, like the frustration of thwarted ambition. Before you know it, you'll come to know anger, fear, and ennui like old friends. Then you'll be ready to relate to kids through the wildfire passions that rule their world. One must have a glimmer of understanding of their plight to do this job at all, much less do it well. Without that understanding, you will be like a tone-deaf conductor, hopelessly flailing around amidst a cacophony of sounds. The first step toward harmony is to forget about what your child is thinking or saying or screaming, and listen to what they're feeling.

Raising children might be an art, but at times it can feel like the art of war due to what David Lynch calls *creativity killers*: interruptions. Your children will interrupt whatever you're doing at maddeningly frequent intervals that seem preternaturally well-timed to destroy any progress you may think that you're achieving. These interruptions will usually be accompanied by the emotional torrents described above. The inconvenience caused by interruptions might sound petty, but a recent study found that such constant interruptions drop your I.Q. by a solid 10 points. So even if you came to this job as an intelligent person, get ready to drop into the slurry of middlebrow humanity.

The fact that the interruptions and inconveniences particular to childcare seem totally unnecessary makes them all the worse. Girl will come to me crying miserably, or Boy will dive into my face with the urgency of a 5-alarm fire, all because of toy trouble. Or I'll hear something smashing on the floor, or water running somewhere, or that clarion call, "Dada! Please wipe me!" Other interruptions are stealthy. If I leave a notebook or an important paper on my desk, it will be scribbled on within seconds. Another one of their favorite pastimes is to pull the bookmark out of every book I try to read. After losing my place a dozen times, I usually give up on ever reading the damn thing. They've made me lose my place in life and in the world, and for that I'm eternally grateful. You have to let the interruptions inform a new approach to life, which will become more like improvisational performance art than an exercise in efficiency. You must first master the art of self-abnegation. Look it up. To good mothers, it comes naturally, but few men can actually surrender themselves to forces beyond their control.

What you've been thinking for several chapters now is correct: making a satire out of the holy duty of child-raising is blasphemy of the worst sort. Yet, I have come to believe that the existence of children is proof of the existence of God, because there is no other way to explain how they survive all the ways they find to put themselves into such mortal danger. They're clearly in the good graces of some mysterious power out there. Maybe the trick is that to them, it's ALL a great mystery. One time I said, "holy mackerel!" But Girl objected, saying "mackerels aren't holy." Boy shot back, "everything is holy!" He's had no traditional religious training that would confine the holy to certain aspects of what we call reality. To them, the word God is just another feeble way that adults try to describe the mystery that is everywhere and in everything, including satirical takes on this job, especially if it removes the taboo of a man doing a good job at it.

"Imagination is not a state. It is human existence itself," William Blake said. Children live the truth of that statement, if you let them. J.M. Barrie let them. Lewis Carroll let them. Mark Twain let them. Along the way, moments of transcendence creep in without your even knowing it. You must watch for them, but you can also try to conjure them. At the end of every day, we welcome Dark Time, the interlude when we turn off the lights, shut the door, and the three of us drift together for a brief moment of communal peace in the Big Bed. Sometimes it lasts only 20 seconds before it crumbles, or sometimes 20 minutes, but however long it may take, the children cherish Dark Time as a decompression from all the hassles of the day, and the perfect prelude to a happy sleep. Even the dog signals his approval by the contented licking of chops in the darkness. Everyone takes a breath. Night is allowed back into our home. With the electrification of our lives, we have lost the night, the darkness, and all it brings--a time of calm, imagination, reflection on the day, and freedom from the pressure to be productive. The night used to be a time of storytelling before the screen squelched that out. But you can at least give darkness its own time and start reclaiming the night, which will then stop being a fearful place for kids. Once you name it, Dark Time, and associate it with calm, much terror will evaporate. When Dark Time is over, I carry each one to their bed and dump them down exactly the way they like it. Boy likes to be dropped hard like a sack of potatoes. Girl likes to be dropped softly from a lesser height, but still with a definitive thud. Sometimes they like me to stay with them while they fall through the threshold of sleep. During the most exhausting years of childcare, Dark Time was often the only time of the day when my befuddlement slipped away.

Boy describes me as a cross between Fred Flintstone and Obi Wan Kinobi. One side is a gruff, unshaven, well-meaning bumbler just trying to get over, while the other is a calm, wise man full of life lessons. I agree. I can be one, and then the other, depending upon whether I am being obeyed or not. Obi Wan says this to SAHDs: at some point, you will ask yourself, what do I have for them? Hopefully this will mean more than baseball or religion or help with math homework or lots of zeros in a bank account. You will wonder whether you have a sliver of poetry left in your soul, because that's what they really need and want—poetry, stories, and different worldviews that can reflect a glimmer of the magic of life. It's also possible you'll discover that's the one thing you want to share with them most of all.

A Fairy Tale of New York

When foreigners at the U.N. ask me what country I'm from, I always tell them: Brooklyn. To our family in those days, Brooklyn was not just a borough of New York City, it was a universe unto itself. We were eight kids crammed into the upstairs of a small two family house in Flatbush. As hard as it might be for an adult to understand, living in a house teeming with other children was paradise. There was always trouble and always fun to share. Brooklyn forced us to live close to one another, and that experience of closeness among so many kids under one roof might have instilled a greater tolerance for the little people somewhere deep in my psyche. The greatest toy any kid can have is another kid, and we had our pick of the best.

On this job, you must try to remember your earliest days. What mattered most to you back then?

My world revolved around black out cakes from Ebinger's bakery, the beach at Riis Park, and St. Jerome's church. Dad was an NYPD Detective. Mom was a Grace Kelly look-alike. Grandmother from Guyana lived with us and prepared all our food Caribbean style. In the winter, the backyard got hosed down and turned into an ice skating rink. In the summer, Flatbush Avenue ran straight into the ocean, and so did we. Artesian wells in a nearby park gave generations of teenagers escape from the watchful eyes of parents. Then Donald Trump's father bought it and paved over the springs to build a Soviet style apartment block, his first moneymaker.

They say that every fortune began with a crime. The elder Trump's crime impoverished an entire neighborhood to enrich a single man. Before long, an atmosphere of menace descended after nightfall. Kids with names like Mary Touhey overdosed in darnk basements. Drugs numbed the bitterness of a crumbling neighborhood for a while, but pretty soon, anyone who could get out did. My parents moved us north of the city, or should I say, my mother forced my father to get us the hell out of there. Brooklyn became a paradise, lost.

It felt like the tribe had disintegrated into suburban space, and for years, all I wanted to do was move back to Flatbush. I badgered my mother, and kept a bag packed and hidden just in case the opportunity arose, or if I decided to take matters into my own 5 year-old hands. If you take care of kids, you must find ways to viscerally remember what it was like to be one. Revisit your earliest connections. Recall what made you happy, what vexed you, and what held magic. You will then have all the tools necessary to live with kids throughout the days and nights without it ruining you or spoiling them.

Postscript: decades after we moved out, the old neighborhood was discovered by another great Island people, the Haitians, who moved in and stabilized the place. Masses at St. Jerome's are now in Creole. Ebinger's has been replaced by Au Beurre Chaud, and Riis Park is full of people enjoying the beach without getting sunburned. Things are okay in Flatbush, once again.

You Have No Idea

Wife and I have an arrangement: she reads all the childcare books and advises me on how to do the job. It works out great. She goes off to her workplace, and I do whatever it takes, none of which you will find in any book, with the possible exception of this one. The first thing Boy did when he learned to read was to devour all the parenting books that his mother bought, rendering them useless by employing the age old strategy, *know thy enemy*. My wife and I have another arrangement: I do 100% of everything. That works out okay too, since trying to divvy up the load resulted in a process of negotiation and ground-truthing so exhausting that nothing actually got done. So if you take this job, be ready to handle it all. Otherwise, give up now, and go chase all the other false gods that society dangles before you, like writing books.

The cumulative stress involved in raising children fulltime cannot be fully imagined or communicated. There is simply no substitute for the experience of dealing with the events of the day, which usually begins with a 2 year screaming in your ear, and ends with the absolute menagerie that is dinnertime. If these experiences don't sound all that hard to deal with, remember that you're reading a book, and not having them. Each and every SAHD or MAHD has been so completely perplexed by their daily labors that they've all made the same statement to their spouses: "you have no idea!" If we weren't so discombobulated by the day's events to even annunciate a full sentence, we would say, "you have no idea of what's involved with performing this job, you haughty windbag! Either do what I say to help out around here, or go to your room." Men have long known about this unspoken ultimatum, and they've repaired to their rooms immediately after dinner.

So expect no sympathy. Wage earners out there in the "work" world feel perfectly justified in complaining about the vagaries and frustrations they face during a day spent with adults. How can you complain about sharing the day with these darling little ones? If you try to explain the difficulties of the day, they will all be found due to your own incompetence and failure to heed expert advice. My point here is that you must not only get used to doing the job, but to also getting criticized for doing it improperly. Salaried women or men find it very difficult to hang up their managerial mindsets when they hit the house. (I prefer the term "salaried women" to "working women" since "working women" suggests that women who care for kids aren't working. I also don't like the term "professional woman" for obvious reasons).

For example, you will be accused of aiding and abetting the kids' raucous fighting because you intervened, against the better knowledge of the experts. Your interference means that they'll never learn to pull themselves out of the vortex of violent discord in which they seem to revel, nevermind the fact that if you allowed harm to come to the kids while they're on your watch, you would be shamed and blamed for the rest of your natural life, and perhaps beyond. Even if Wife is the one who left the tiger balm within toddler reach, or if the 6 year-old plunged his sister under water in the bath, it is always your fault. She will then leave a brochure for anger management on the kitchen table and order you to read it. I have found that imitating Buster Keaton's blank face is the only possible response at these moments. As usual, things will get worse from there.

Wife will begin expecting treatment at a level equivalent to the care you provide to the kids. If you can find their shoes, surely you can find hers. If you can cook special meals for them, certainly you can prepare whatever fad diet she's on this week. If you can clean up after them, then you damned well can do it for her. Get the picture? You have no idea.

Perhaps you think that you can game the system by doing a somewhat poor job of things in the hope she'll no longer trust you with the tasks at hand, and take many of them over herself. If your kids are always clean, well-fed and organized, she'll think you have way too much time on your hands. Let them get a little dirty and hungry and disheveled. Likewise, you might want to let yourself slide a bit. Leave their snot on your pants until she complains about the dirty sweats you're always wearing. She'll see such signs and begin to get an idea of what you do at work. Then, when she gets angry at the apparent deterioration in the state of domestic affairs, whip out that anger management brochure and brandish it in her face. I'm sure she'll calmly take it and pledge to abide by all the helpful insights contained therein. However, this will occur after she smacks you across the face with it and blows her top. There is no winning the illogical game. Return to the strategy elaborated in paragraph one of this section.

If you have gotten this far, congratulations are in order. We can assume that you're successfully weathering the gales of child-control. It is now time to have your humanity and grip on sanity put to the acid test. Workplace frustrations are usually visited upon members of the household when the wage-slave returns and struts about the house, a little bottle of nitroglycerin in the guise of a puffed-up sovereign surveying his or her kingdom. One day soon, those frustrations will boil over when your mate returns from work, irate due to circumstances beyond your control, and spits out the following three incendiary words. "I'm supporting you!" You, as the child-rearing drudge, will look up from cooking dinner, changing diapers, washing the dishes, or doing the laundry, and realize that your mate cannot see the obvious irony of the situation. Who is supporting whom, exactly? Here, we once again find ourselves in thrall to the cultural brainwashing that time equals money and money is all that counts. *Good Housekeeping* magazine will never clue their blissful readers into what frequently happens next. The offended party might employ one of the kitchen implements they were washing to reduce the haughty offender to a lump of protoplasm. The break-out moment for women's liberation was beautifully illustrated in the scene from *2001: A Space Odyssey* when the ape discovers that a thigh bone can smash a skull. That discovery had a wonderful equalizing effect in the war of the sexes--an enraged woman could brain her husband just as easily as he could brain her. She didn't need to listen to her old man's insults anymore. She could just off him in his sleep, and move on to a more enlightened ape mate. The women's liberation movement is as old as evolution itself.

Which reminds me of a cautionary tale my Dad told me about how one of his NYPD detectives was awakened in the middle of the night by the sound of click...click...click. He opened his eyes to find himself staring down the barrel of his own snub-nosed .38 Detective Special. His wife was pulling the trigger over and over again, expecting rapid relief from offensive treatment. She had no doubt endured some final insult that pushed her over her limit, but unbeknownst to her, the cop had emptied all of the bullets out before going to bed. How many other wives would have killed their husbands by now if nice little handguns were within easy reach? I dare say we'd be looking at holocaust type numbers. All because of the enslavement of bread makers by bread winners. The money-winning spouse has suffered degrading treatment at the hands of whatever sacrificial system they endure in the workplace, and they must unload some it onto the one who remains at home. This behavior occurs regardless of whether the man or the woman works at home with the kids.

"Slave" is defined as a human being who is owned as property by another and is absolutely subject to his or her will. In this light, the modern woman's liberation movement was actually a slave revolt. But like most revolutions, it turned out to be an ingenious trap, because they revolted right into the hands of the economic system that enslaved them in the first place. Even when revolutions are successful, there is often a return to the status quo once the dust settles. Women can easily replace men in the workplace, but that changes nothing. Modern culture has been wildly successful at ingraining the notion that the world is divided into the realm of money-earners, and the purgatorio of those who are reliant upon the kindness of money-earners. So, no, women were not liberated. They simply traded one set of shackles for another.

Women should have revolted and over-turned the system entirely. Imagine a world of worker-owned cooperatives, rather than corporations owned by the rich. Women would have not only liberated themselves, they would have liberated men, too. I can see the web blogs bubbling with vitriol already: did you read that kook? See what happens when a man takes care of the children?

Perhaps it would be a more realistic goal to envision a matriarchy of the 1950s sci-fi movie variety, with blondes in shiny mid-riffs ruling over scared and subservient men. Befitting the dogs that we are at heart, men would be fitted with steel collars that clamp down whenever we disobey. Let's face it, we were always putty in their hands anyway. Remember that Star Trek episode where Kirk must wear such a collar? That would be us, and the remote controls would be in the hands of women. We'd be fed steak and cheesecake and given all the sexual favors we could possibly need, but if we ever got bigger ideas, that charming little choker would tighten accordingly. Women would live in peace and harmony, equally sharing the wealth, that is, until one of them fell hard for one of us. Then the wars would restart overnight and we'd be right back where we started. So, disregard the foregoing stratagem, and let's move to a deeper level, shall we?

In the old days, women were spiritually superior to men, probably because they were on the job. When the yoke of caring for children, and for husbands who act like children, became too stultifying, women threw it off and became just like us— spiritual dolts with short fuses all "leaning-in" to their careers. Women used to work in the fields of life's eternal cycle, and revel in the secret pleasure of nearness to cosmic regeneration, at least when they weren't screaming at their 2 year–olds. It's like they were angels who suddenly fell in love with money or careers or whatever you want to call it, and in the bargain had to forfeit their supernatural powers. Vanquished at last! Now they're in position to reverse polarity with us—and be the all-powerful sole breadwinners. My guess is that most men will not be brave and secure enough to handle it. We're too stewed in the lust for power to find the humility that's key to that particular kingdom; too bamboozled by the time=money equation to slow down and catch a glimpse of the eternity radiating out of our children's eyes. If the male caretaker has not yet been experienced and spiritually uplifted, the little boat of marital harmony will capsize when the women tells him that she supports him, dumping both lost sailors into the fathomless sea of single parenthood.

And so, the question of whether you are both living in a satisfyingly reciprocal system of support must be asked and answered on a regular basis. Just remember that you have no idea what the other party is going through.

8 ½

Today at 8:30 in the morning, I stood alone in a vacant schoolyard battling an overwhelming urge to laugh and cry at the same time. The day had come at long last when both kids were old enough for school. I dropped off my third grader, then turned around and dropped off the kindergartener. The door closed, and they were both gone. A huge surge of relief swept over me and poured into a strange emptiness. I had just finished an eight-year long slog through tantrums, dangers, dirty diapers, feedings, and all the rest, and I had my life back. But the kids had performed a judo move on me by becoming my life. It was a black comedy, an appalling situation that was really very funny. The cauldron of childcare had melted down my old identity, but it was not yet poured into a new shape. That poor identity thief who stole me must have been very confused by the goods he had in his satchel.

When your kids reach 8½, which is about halfway to the time when they'll leave the nest for college, you'll find yourself inside 8½, the Fellini film about a director who's trying to make a movie but no longer knows the story he wants to tell. A similar conundrum can also appear halfway through life, or halfway through writing a book like this one. Years on the childcare circuit accelerate as they unfold, and you get overtaken. The days become surreal blurs racing by at lightening speed. With no time to do anything but the necessities, I entered a stage of drift, where the constant work evaporates whatever sense of direction appeared to exist. The work is so consuming that it'll be over and the kids grown before you even know what's happened.

Kids know to wait until you find yourself in this stupor before they pop the big unanswerable question that you must answer. "Dad, why do we have to die?" They want the heart of this enigma laid bare in the simplest of terms. The job has aged you faster than a firefly, and they can see it. They know that death will get you, and they want to know why. Hopefully, this is a sign that you've been doing a good job and they want you to stick around awhile longer, or at least until they reach adolescence. At that point you will become an impossible burden who is better off dead.

I see now that religion was invented in part to feed you nice pat answers that can be regurgitated to your kids when you can't bear to look stumped after they confront you with impossible questions. Can I tell them that without death, without some ending, this voyage through time would not be a voyage at all, but some eternal prank? No, that perspective will have to wait for them to discover for themselves, probably with some help from Samuel Beckett. So I told them that death is how the Earth renews itself. True, but very unsatisfactory from the point of view of a 7 or 8 year old who's petrified of death, who's looking for a simple definition of the word, DEATH, who just wants to know, is it the final end--is that all there is? I'm sure that there are countless witty and wise philosophical answers that I could crib from the glut of spiritual how-to books out there, but I try not to utter phony tropes.

"No one knows," I said, "death is a mystery we all live with. It's a reminder to keep focused on the here and now." That answer made perfect sense to the kids, and they headed off to enjoy the moment.

Be ready for your kids to continue asking the deepest questions ever pondered by humans, and also voicing the deepest truths. How did space/time begin? How do you know everything isn't alive? Did you know that water is alive? Atom bombs are really pretty simple. Why didn't they give the Japanese a warning? Dad, what did you like to do most when you were 8? Did your parents ever beat you? When you were a kid, what did you want to do when grew up? Did you ever try pot? Oftentimes, the seemingly simple questions they ask illuminate the complexity of the world they're trying to grasp. I once asked Boy what he'd like to study over the summer between second and third grade. "How a spider spins a web," he said. I realized that a full and true answer to that question could form the core of a complete educational experience through a PhD. degree and beyond. It would have to include biology, ecology, chemistry, mathematics, geometry, design, engineering, evolutionary theory, meteorology, cosmology, and anthropology, to name a few. There is really no end to the connections linked by that web— the original, real, functional web. A fully integrated answer would also have to include the philosophical truth: we're all working in a mysterious partnership with the universe, in which we are the partial authors, no more, no less, of the reality that we're perceiving and living. The other author is a mystery, no matter who says they have the answer. Raising a child is like studying a spiderweb, it takes you everywhere you might want to go, and plenty of places you never imagined existed.

In the end, maybe the your specific answers to their questions aren't what matters most. Maybe all that matters is your attitude. We just buried our dog who kept sentry duty every night for 17 years by pacing from one kid's bed to the other. We all howled at the moon during his midnight burial in the backyard. He was a champion of all the qualities you would want your kids to emulate. Forget the latest flavor in child rearing perspicacity that's going around. Get a great dog instead, train it well, and let it teach your kids what's important, like fidelity, friendship, curiosity, freedom, love of the outdoors, and living in the here and now.

The Three Amigos

One night a long time ago, three kids huddled against a mountainside in a tiny shelter they built out of sticks and leaves and mud. Inside, the smell of Earth was as strong as a freshly dug grave. Their body heat would bring up the temperature just enough to avoid freezing to death overnight. Our little tribe could survive anything. Even the collapse of civilization wouldn't pose much of a problem. In the dark of that snug Earthen cocoon, we talked about how much fun it would be to revert back to being hunter/gatherers, which we figured would make more sense than trying to deal with the blind stupidity of the adult society we were about to enter.

After high school, Ed, Jerry and I went our separate

ways. Ed excelled in math and he continued on with it in college. Jerry picked up his father's axe as a New York City fireman. I went to Florida to study marine science. We'd run into each other from time to time and reconfirm our continued outsidership from the mainstream, even as we found ourselves swimming in it. They got married young and had kids. To support them, Ed would take the high-speed elevator up to the 92nd floor of the World Trade Center's North Tower where he worked as a futures trader. Jerry used his crazy courage to build a heroic record, until a stairwell in a burning Bronx apartment house collapsed under him. His medical leave included treatment to dry out from the drugs and alcohol he had always enjoyed.

Jerry showed up at my brother's wake looking good. He'd been in A.A. for years and seemed solidly grounded in the sober life. Ed was the only adult male there, my father and brothers included, who was shedding tears for the loss of Brian, my charismatic younger brother. He had tried to withdraw from a bad Vodka habit on his own, but had a seizure instead that took his life in the same bed in which he was conceived. A couple of weeks earlier, I'd had a vivid dream in which I met Ed on a commuter train. The seats were full of people, and I was walking toward the back of the car when I met him, standing near the rear door with a look of terrible sadness in his eyes. I told Ed about my dream at the wake, and said it might have foreshadowed Brian's death, but the strange thing is how the feeling augured something even worse.

Chris Peters is a traditional spiritual practitioner from the Karok tribe of Northern California who would stay at my apartment on his trips to New York. On one of his visits, he asked me to take him up to the observation deck atop the World Trade Center. I'd lived in the shadow of those towers for most of my life, but never bothered to take a trip to the roof. When Chris and I walked out into the sky one hundred and eleven stories above Manhattan, we looked down at the city far below us, and saw how all the man-made construction looked unreal from the height, like a model, or a virtual overlay of some type. Only the natural features seemed real: Central Park, the waterways surrounding the city, the harbor, and the ocean beyond. Chris said some words in his Native language and let a small clump of tobacco float down over the edge of the platform. I'd seen him perform this blessing before in other places out West that the tribes consider sacred.

I watched that tower burn to the ground while holding my infant son in my arms. Ed never saw his four kids again. Jerry was not on duty that day, but he burst into tears when he saw the towers fall because he was well aware of how many of his colleague's lives went down with them. I was worried that the disastrous loss might challenge his sobriety. He reassured me by saying that, "they took all those guys down. What am I going to do? Let them take me down, too?" It was meant to be a rhetorical question, but he would become another victim of 9/11, when only 18 months later, a slurry of drugs and alcohol sucked him under, leaving two young sons behind.

Watching those two skyscrapers peel down to the ground like illusions crumbling into dust made a lot of us think hard about what's really important. Loss always awaits us all. Ed and Jerry brought home the reality that I could lose my children, or they could lose me, at any moment. The deaths of my best childhood friends, together with the death of my brother, gave me an appreciation for this brief life that informs my every decision. The three strikes I described earlier might have put me in this job, but these three amigos keep me here. If they were granted another moment of life, they'd spend it with their kids and families. I've chosen to live mine accordingly, even if it appears that I can't afford to do so financially. It's easy to lose perspective in modern America. Just remember that death is always there to remind you what's important.

Attack of the Indigo Children

Beware, for kids with otherworldly powers roam among us. They can't help the fact that they were born benighted, special, and better than other kids. Just ask their parents. They'll tell you that their little dictator is in fact an "Indigo Child" who can see angels, read your mind, and predict the future because they're superior beings. The books and websites and DVDs that spout this nonsense seem blissfully unaware that the new age is over, thank the Goddess. Children who claim to be "Indigo" are different only in their ability to be above-average annoying. In the old days, we called this syndrome the "my child is God's gift to the world" delusion. But then, as now, criticizing the behavior of another person's dog or kid remains a transgression that will not be tolerated by those who need to hear it most. Indigo parents will see nothing wrong with their kid jumping another kid, because theirs' is, you know, gifted with a special holiness. The books and websites that promote the Indigo Child concept should all be retitled: "How to Raise a Fake Psychic Spoiled Brat."

I see this phenomenon as the flip side of the devil-child movie genre that peaked during the height of the baby boom in the early 60s, when it must have seemed that children were taking over the world. Adults have always feared kids, and projected our own demons and angels upon them. One British film from the 60's called "Children of the Damned" captured the exploits of supernaturally evil children with glowing white eyes who could kill an adult through the shear power of their minds. The military got called in to exterminate the kids once they had all been corralled into a church. Stories of tiny people who can dominate grownups, such as the Liliputians who can tie you up and tie you down, are true fictions because children do just that. You're a monstrous giant with super powers ruling their world, and as a potential existential threat, you must be dealt with proactively. We are the Captain Hooks and they are the Peter Pans. We are avaricious bad guys and they are noble upholders of freedom and all that is good. We want to enslave them. They must defeat us. The part missing from these myths is the need to show kids the importance of losing and how to take it. Being able to honestly evaluate the lessons offered by losing is key to becoming a genuine human being. It will also lead to winning, and hopefully, winning with humility. Their imaginations and identities must be grounded in the understanding that living in the real world demands consideration for others. Otherwise, you will be raising a child who is not only delusional, but is both entitled and delusional. These are the children whom we should rightfully fear as they grow into adults, and their parents are the ones who're damned.

Some sage once said that the two most important things that you can give a child are roots and wings. Am I too far along to take some random piece of advice seriously? Indulge me a moment while I try... Roots? Okay, root them in their families, in both their human family and their Earth family. Give them wings? Wrong. They have wings already. Just don't clip them, or allow schools or stupid peer groups to clip them. There's a line between preserving a kid's imagination and dispelling flights of fantasy that can border on hallucinations. They don't have to become Indigo children to see the way toward a better future. We only have to respect their righteous observations, play along now and then with their fantasies of empowerment, and bring them back to reality when they entertain visions of infallibility and domination. Or you can just sign them up for a sports team and let the realities of competition do the work for you.

Rabid Sports Fans

The youth wrestling team coach performed an anxiety-ridden, Kabukiesque performance while watching his little wrestler grapple with an opponent out on the mat. He shouted, jumped, pirouetted, covered his eyes, jabbed the air, twisted his arms, and ran his fingers through his hair in feverish distraction at missed opportunities. I witnessed the entire litany of human gestural communications, representing all the pageantry of life, compressed into a solo display by a man who had no idea that he was even on stage. It was as if he were wearing a virtual reality suit and trying to telegraph the movements of his diminutive avatar. The poor, overwrought coach died a thousand deaths, punctuated by fits of hopeful redemption, until his final resurrection and ascension into heaven came when his boy won the match. Never before had I witnessed such jubilation.

Maybe this is just the way that sports are done in New Jersey, or maybe it's part of a larger phenomenon. Either way, some fathers are getting a little out of control, spending all of their time and money on organized kids sports. Why have people turned what were supposed to be fun endeavors into semi-pro ordeals? Are they expecting payback when their kid gets a college scholarship or a multimillion dollar contract in the pros? Is it the hope for prestige and hero worship that might be bestowed on their kid, and by extension, onto themselves? Apparently, it's now unacceptable to let kids just go out, make some friends, get some exercise, and have some fun on their own. I think we're in trouble, here, Dads. Sports are a good thing, and for some energetic kids, a mandatory thing, but too much of a good thing equals a bad thing.

In my old neighborhood, the sport of choice up until age 14 was simple: kill the carrier, which was also known as "Salugi." No matter what other sport we started out playing, it would always devolve into Salugi. (Who the hell was Salugi, anyway?). There were no coaches, no techniques, no referees, no equipment, neither field nor boundaries of any sort, and perhaps most importantly, no parents. If parents had been around, they would have certainly broken up what appeared to them to be the craziest, all-against-one scapegoating gang fight ever witnessed. The game had one simple object: to kill whoever was brave or dumb enough to pick up the football and run for their lives.

When the carrier was caught, which was always inevitable, the pile-ons were epic, with nine or ten kids diving one atop the other until the air would be crushed out of the poor ball carrier underneath them all. The pressure would build until the ball would come squirting out of the bottom, unleashing yet another crazed scramble to see who would be the first to scoop it up. Copping a jagged adrenaline rush is the only reason that I can fathom why anyone would want to pick up that ball and try to outrun a rabid pack of sweaty, wild-eyed adolescent boys who would eventually catch up with you and kill you. But what a sport! It was totally elemental, engaged the gamut of emotions, and required no adult supervision. Another reason we loved Salugi is that it was just like life--no one ever won. Despite its apparent ultra-violence, nobody ever got hurt or even lost their temper playing it, probably because Salugi was like one enormous fight, in which everyone took turns getting their asses kicked. People got hurt playing football and baseball and got into fights playing basketball, but Salugi was our game, and injuries were not permitted.

Today, television has transformed sports into something more akin to religions. They have their chants, their sacred animals, their holy colors, their numerologies, their saints and sinners, their immutable rules, and so on. It all conspires to relieve parents of any perspective they might have had on the importance of organized athletics. They end up pouring all of their kid's time into sports even if they're failing subjects at school, or in trouble outside of it. Sometimes, this goes on for years until things become desperate, and like an overextended gambler who must play his last dime, they pour even more into their kid's sports. Then Dad ends up having an illiterate drop-out who never even made it to the college level, much less the pros, all because Budweiser commercials and the NFL/MLB/NBA/NHL made him do it.

The answer to why Dads get suckered into such nonsense might lie in a scientific study showing that men who voted for a losing candidate had their testosterone levels measurably drop. They ended up feeling significantly more submissive, unhappy and generally grumpy. The testosterone effect occurred as if they had personally gone head to head in a tilted contest for dominance. Fathers get so worked up over their kid's games because it can seem as if their own manhood's are on the line. Hence, it becomes easy to lose sight of the cold hard fact that all of the great breakthroughs in the history of humankind came only after serial failures, and that sports may be the best way to teach children how to face it. Sports can give invaluable life lessons, but only if parents don't bring their own baggage to the games.

Kids need and want to learn how to react to losing, which means they need a mentor who can show, mainly by their behavior, that it is okay to lose. Failure is just the flipside of winning, and a good coach gives that message to his players while also getting the best out of them. It is a fine but clear line to walk. True winners become winners only by going through the emotional gauntlet of losing and losing again. True coaches are good only to the degree to which they're mentors who can show kids the value of both winning and loosing.

Over the weekend, I watched a little league game in which my 9 year-old son was playing his first season. He'd been struggling to escape the clutches of a mean slump, and I could barely look when he took the plate with bases loaded in a tied game in extra innings. To raise the tension even higher, he fouls one off, and then lets a strike go by. The final pitch came in, and he crushed the ball for a game-winning grand slam. The crowd went wild. He got the game ball and the title of MVP, none of which would have meant anything had he not overcome all kinds of obstacles along the way. Sports can help to hone the art of dealing with pinnacles and valleys, which is so important to having a stable life.

While I'm on the subject of sports, here's a trick question: is the surface of the Earth covered mostly by playing fields, ball courts, or water? Yes, we do live on a planet called Earth, but of course, it's not covered mostly by earth at all, but by water. So doesn't it make sense to consider swimming the most important sport for your kid to master? It should be considered a basic activity, like walking or playing video games. Parents should take it one step further and sign their kids up for a youth swimming team for at least two or three years. That will increase their chances of survival on this ocean planet ten fold, plus open up the world of water for them to explore. After becoming amphibian, they might even begin to value their home planet and decide that it is worth saving. You never know. It worked for me.

Little Women

As long as one of the little people in your orbit is a female, you will be rewarded for your troubles by having a girl adore you as no woman ever has nor ever will. Why just this morning, I knew how it felt to be Paul McCartney circa 1965, for I had a beautiful girl clamped around my leg, begging me not to leave her, and bawling her poor heart out. She couldn't care less that it was in a public place with many onlookers, or that her babysitter was waiting with open arms. I had to leave because the rest of the world does not recognize me as a rock star, and circumstances were forcing me to sell some of my time. None of that harsh reality gave Girl any comfort. I started to gently pry my biggest little fan off of my leg, but she slid down to my ankle, tightened her grip, and hung on tenaciously, single-minded in her devotion to her one and only man/god. If you take this job, prepare yourself for the unbridled adulation that comes with the territory.

Seeing me struggling with Girl at the playground one day, an Hispanic mother offered true words of support, "you can talk to boys and persuade them to do what you want, but girls are born *little women*," and we all know what immovable objects women can be. My Girl will automatically do the opposite of whatever I ask her to do, despite her undying love for me, or more accurately, because of her undying love for me. She must maintain her independence, and go along with me because she chooses to do so, not out of duress, which would suggest that she doesn't love me as much as she does. Maybe that's why women are so maddeningly and wonderfully uncontrollable.

There's no mystery about what women want. They want their own way, and the first thing they discover is that they can get their own way by locking themselves in the bathroom and doing whatever it is they do in there. It might start with combining spot remover with moisturizer to create a new brand of toothpaste, or painting their clothes with white-out and markers. These experiments always end years later with complicated beauty treatments. At age seven, Girl is fully capable of putting on elegant make-up, selecting a tasteful and fashionable ensemble with matching jewelry, and asking to be taken out to an upscale restaurant. She's received no schooling on these activities, for her instinct comes as part of her birthright. Wife never wears makeup, her jewelry is usually limited to her wedding ring, and her fashion sense is, well, unconventional. Meanwhile, Girl loves every manner of face paint, nail polish, wigs, perfumes, and fashion accessories. In so many ways, girls are indeed women already, and women are indeed different.

If you have a girl, you will send her up to get ready for bed, then go up there 20 minutes later to discover that the only thing changed is a new coat of nail polish smeared all over her fingertips. Glitter nail polish, that is, made in China for extra adhesion and toxicity, given as a gift for her attendance at some birthday party and secreted away in her clothing where it could not be found and confiscated by the authorities. One night she found a magazine ad for a diamond encrusted Tag Heur watch that impressed her so profoundly that she brought it to me and asked if I would buy her one. She will admire Cartier advertisements, and unfailingly select the piece of jewelry so extravagant that it's marked "price upon request." One night, she brought forth an advertisement for a luxurious custom kitchen, and asked if we could change ours to look like that one, "because it's beautiful." At eight, she asked me, "Dad, can we spend the night in a hotel on my birthday, a nice hotel in the city, and go to a Broadway play with a couple of my friends?" We've never had such an evening, but these sensibilities come hard-wired in females regardless of their age, ethnicity, or any other subcategory you can dream up. I replied that I was thinking more in the line of pizza and a movie. She came back with the compromise of toasting s'mores in front of the fireplace with her friends, which would be another first. I said yes, then almost burned down the house when a chimney fire turned our flue into a jet engine. The kids loved the thrill of having such a hazardous, unplanned event punctuating the party. My attempts to economize and inject a dose of reality into the birthday party craze backfired--her original idea of a big night out in New York would have been cheaper in the end. Women operate according to a wisdom that is out of our reach. Defy it at your own peril.

Another change-up that Girl brings to our household is a love of the holidays. Weeks before each one, the requests start pouring in. "We need to put up decorations, Dad, inside and out! We need to get ready," for Halloween, Thanksgiving, Christmas, Easter, the dog's birthday, the Super Bowl, etc. If I say not yet, she'll be down in the basement dragging the stuff out anyway. Special baking must get down. People need to be invited over. The dog needs a costume, and so on. We never did these things when she was very young—the sudden need for them bloomed atavistically from her female mind at around age 4. When I look into her hopeful, happy eyes, the essential things somehow get done, even though I get little or no help in these endeavors from Boy or Wife. The Halloween party happens. The tree gets decorated. Eggs get colored. And we're all better off because of it. I see now that women drew us out of living in caves by demanding a better way of life. They required a brighter world. When the house sparkles around Christmas or it's filled with ghouls at Halloween or the pastel spring colors of Easter, life has been rounded into a celebratory structure, and a glass of wine never tasted so good. Thank you women, even if you forced me to do it.

At 2am this morning, after settling Girl down from a walking nightmare, Warren Zevon's lyrics played in my head. "She's all grown up, she's got a young man waiting." I've been up a couple of times every night for several years now to calm nightmares, and I'm feeling more than a tad worn down, but Warren's song came as a gift that reminds me that in the blink of an eye, she'll be on her own. The very idea of it caused a wave of what I call clairvoyant nostalgia. I project myself into the future and get a sense for how special these days will seem after they're gone. Luckily, Girl did me the service of dispelling that feeling in the morning when she refused to cooperate with anything that needed to get done. It was such a maddening moment that I actually looked forward to her achieving full emancipation.

Just keep in mind that although you're a SAHD, you're still a gruff beast, and if you have a baby daughter and plan to raise her to adulthood, you will use the "B" word, perhaps no more than once, but out it will slip, I assure you. Forgive yourself immediately and move on. In fact, you will use another "B" word if you have a son. Do likewise. Enough said.

Great Expectations

Career guidance in my family was considered something that only God could provide, and his job was easy since your choices were limited to cop, nurse, or if you really wanted to be radical and start trouble, a fireman. Seeking anything of higher status would have been considered pure hubris and a probable path to hell. The choice of what to do for a living was considered a low-level decision, an after-thought that had nothing to do with who we were as human beings or the kind of person that we would become. Fate and necessity, those other names for the God of a good Catholic, would drop us into a certain size hole whether we were suited to it by natural inclination or not. Education was turned over to God, who appeared in the guise of nuns, to whom we were bequeathed at a tender age. Looking back on it now, my upbringing might have been the perfect psychological preparation for the job of being a Baby Wrestler. Accept what life offers, don't strive too hard, and try not to use curse words.

Somehow, I ended up on several fast tracks at different times in my life, but sooner or later, each time I reverted back to type.

Parents' approach to education and career choices for their children now verges on the maniacal. Even Catholic schools have followed the lead of expensive private schools, with well-off parents focused on producing well-paid offspring. The grammar school I attended, Our Lady Of Fatima, charged the miracle price of only $200 per child a year. The nuns were free labor back then, there was no technology, and student needs were simple: to be the chosen ones who were selected to raise an enormous white dust cloud by clapping the erasers free of chalk at the end of the day. To the nuns, all that really mattered was to develop kids' innate sense for doing the right thing, and for thinking of themselves as the kind of people who do it. Sports were a fine distraction, but far from the pseudo-pro activities that they are today. The craze of college sports, driven by the great Satan, television, had yet to trickle down their big money and prestige to the Catholic high schools. Once those schools had churned out enough Wall Street millionaires, though, everything changed. The magic of money supplanted the magic of some dirt poor Rabbi who wandered the desert a couple of thousand years ago. Catholic high schools now charge $15,000/year and up, and their sports teams are tops in the country. It's no longer enough for them to focus on turning out people of good conscience, because then the alumni would never be able to afford to send their kids to Catholic school.

I don't mean to suggest that everyone who has an early idea of their professional direction in life is a bad person. At age six, Wife knew that she wanted to be a scientist, and never wavered from that goal. For a while, she tried pressuring our kids into deciding, by second grade, what they wanted to be when they grew up. She would hit them with the question every day, until Boy came up with an answer that put her badgering to rest. "I want to be a millionaire playboy," he said gravely one morning. She never asked again. Although initially meant as a joke, the career choice that he had hit upon began to grow in his imagination until most other options seemed rather inferior by comparison. Maybe the nuns had the right approach after all. When I was a grade schooler, and for some time afterwards, I considered nuns to be a strange pestilence on my life and on the lives of my fellows, but I now see some of the wisdom of these women who had no children, but considered all children to be their own.

Still, there must exist a balance somewhere in the universe whereby a parent can refrain from pressuring their kid to make a premature choice of profession while remaining alert to signs that they might be leaning in some general direction. Girl recently discovered my old tripod in the basement and developed such a fascination with it that she is upstairs taking a nap with it at this very moment. We took this cue and bought her a cheap digital camera. Both kids are now taking still life photos, and like all kids, they're creative geniuses, except that Boy now states with conviction that he wants to be a wrestler in the morning and a boxer in the afternoon—basically fighting from dawn till dusk. Girl believes that she's a pop diva in the making, but she silences her medical Mom by telling her that she wants to be doctor. To prove the point, she loves chasing Boy around the house with a toy syringe threatening to administer a painful shot. Although it's true that she's a creative dynamo who's constantly producing new material in all the art forms, her main goal is to just stay with me forever. Not much of a future in that one, but it does make me feel like I'm getting a passing grade for the job.

The Used Couch that Sent Me to Italy

Traveling with children requires careful planning, especially regarding the dosages required to safely knock them out cold in a crowded conveyance as a measure of last resort. I don't take the responsibility for planning and executing our family sojourns lightly, which is why Wife's idea of going to Italy sounded absolutely preposterous. The kids didn't want to go either, but she was headed there for a professional conference, and since her expenses were covered, Wife wanted the family to join her regardless of the additional cost involved. I pointed out that it would take about three years to pay off such an adventure, even on our usual shoestring travel budget. I did not mention my rough calculation as to how many years such a trip would likely take off my life, but that was another good reason why I managed to keep the idea in the negative category, until, that is, I made the mistake of bringing home a used couch without spousal consent. Don't ever do that.

My error put me at a considerable disadvantage during the ensuing commotion. Wife recognized the power imbalance immediately, and exploited it to her full advantage by insisting, as a prerequisite to reconciliation, that I fly over with the kids to meet her in Italy. It was an offer that I could not refuse. The second-hand denim couch had suddenly turned into a magical flying sofa bent on taking me to far-off lands whether I wanted to go or not. My initial shock and disbelief slowly turned into grudging acceptance, and I plunged into preparing an ambitious itinerary that embraced the entire northern tier of Italy. We'd cover Milan, Verona, Venice, Cinque Terra, and Lake D'Orta, all on a non-existent budget. I did everything in my power to ensure that things would go smoothly, or at least, not terribly awry. I even took the kids down to the Italian tourism office in Rockefeller Center to get copies of all the printed materials they had in stock. I studied maps like the general of an invading army, called Italian friends for advice, sifted through accommodation options, and made the cheapest possible nonrefundable reservations for the flight, hotels across our route, and a rental car. All this prep work was done while I was under extreme pressure to write a policy paper for the 2010 General Assembly, perform the most ambitious renovation work I had ever done on our house, and shepherd a first grader and a fourth grader through the start of their school year. Never do that, either.

When the day came, Wife left for Italy, and I got serious about prepping everything for our trip to join her in Verona a few days later. On the morning of our departure, I discovered that Boy's only pair of sneakers had disintegrated around his feet, and that his face was blooming with red streaks from a poison ivy rash. I can now see that these developments were faint messages from the near future that despite my meticulous planning, things might not go so swimmingly after all. Ignorant of these inklings at the time, and with only one boss in the picture, I proceeded with a high degree of confidence in my ability to surmount whatever minor challenges might arise.

At the JFK international terminal, the kids and I were stunned by the length of the serpentine line of travelers awaiting check in. We cued up, and the kids soon discovered the great fun of pulling down the red velvet ropes, fighting viciously in tight quarters, and bumping into other travelers as we snaked along the seemingly endless line. At the very moment of my breaking point when none of us could endure another second of waiting, we were called forth to the ticketing machine. I don't like those machines, and a mutual dislike was confirmed when it refused to cooperate. Then a harried human attendant took over and swiped our passports through the machine. My enmity for that dumb computer seemed justified when even she had trouble making it work. Then she checked the kids' passports and uttered words that shall remain in infamy: "they expired last April. See? They cannot travel with these passports."

The five stages of death and dying blitzed through me in 45 seconds. I went from rejection, "no, it can't be right," to anger "goddamn!" to bargaining "please change things," to the depths of depression "the gods have betrayed me," and finally to an acceptance of our fate, which Girl sealed with the sad question, "you mean we're not going to Italy?" Wife had checked the passports herself before she left, but missed the fact that children's passports expire after only 5 years. How fast can five years go? This job compresses time like no other. The inscrutable machine had won.

Divine intervention seemed our only hope as we stood there, stunned and unable to move from the head of the line. Sure enough, an angel appeared in the guise of a young female baggage handler who cracked open a tiny ray of sunlight. "You can try going down to Philadelphia and pleading your case to the Customs Department. I'll book you on the same flight tomorrow night." We got out of line and staggered toward the exit. The bags that I had hefted with ease moments before were suddenly 3 times heavier. My heart rate rose 30 beats per minute above normal and stayed that way for the next 48 hours. The bewildered kids were all over me with beseeching requests to simply go to Italy, right now, even as we got in line for a yellow cab for the ride home. Whatever magical powers that old couch possessed had turned evil. It was about to suck up all of the money and the time I'd put into making the trip happen.

I hit the house in full mission impossible mode. I'd been there before on various missions overseas with the U.N., so I set up a command center, downloaded the government forms, and arranged a special appointment the next morning at the Customs office in Philly. My hopes were soaring, but they sank when I read the fine print on the passport renewal form: both parents would have to be present during a rush passport renewal. I would have to write an explanation for some extraordinary circumstance that prevented one of us from being there. I worked through until 5am, when it was time to get the kids up for the trip to the city of brotherly love. Boy wanted to watch a movie on the portable DVD player with Girl in the backseat. That sounded like a good idea to keep them from fighting, especially if I was going to navigate unfamiliar roadways. Yes, I would harness technology in the service of mankind.

As we approached Philly, technology turned on me once again. The DVD player made Girl carsick, and she threw up all over herself. I pulled into a Dunkin Donuts parking lot, peeled off her vomit-soaked tights, and wiped down her legs with baby wipes. I removed the rubber mat from under her feet and dumped it upside down in a rain puddle to wash off the puke. Meanwhile,

Boy had begun pacing in front of the store, saying, "I have a terrible stomach ache. Worst ever." Great. Two sick kids now, one with nasty red streaks of poison ivy on his face, making him look like he was swiped by a werewolf. Time to ignore all that, make a bathroom run, and get everybody buckled back in for a hair-raising drive into the morning rush hour traffic over bridges, through tunnels, and down old streets to our inner city destination: the Customs house near Constitution Square, only to find that it's closed for another hour. The parking spot I snagged seemed too good to be true, and I suspected that the confusing and contradictory signage would result in the car being towed, sinking any chance we had left of Italy. But it turns out that the Philly displays such signage for the pure fun of baffling you, unlike New York, where it is cheese in a car-sized mousetrap.

An hour or so with two young kids can begin languorously enough, but it always ends with a frantic search for a toilet. In such extremis, I sought the advise of Park Rangers, and we made a bee-line for the only public toilet nearby while I chanted the mantra, "you'll make it! You'll make it!" And we did, only to be met by a group of elderly Chinese tourists whose baleful looks told a sad tale: all facilities were padlocked for another half hour. I was now faced with an emergency within the larger emergency. Stress was heaped upon stress, seeking to find the straw that would break me. I rushed back to the Ranger, who pointed out a building two blocks away that might have an open restroom. Each step of those two blocks brought pleas and convictions that things could not be held any longer. Prayers went out to the bathroom demigod, beseeching that deity to keep sphincters closed and the bathroom open until we got there. At the very end of their limits, both kids were embraced by a rare kindness from that otherwise inscrutable totem.

When we returned to the Customs House, we encountered a long line of impatient people trying to get through the metal detectors and into the building. Inside the passport room, cued up on another hideous line, giving the kids still more irresistible chances to act badly. After an interminable wait, we approached the window where a woman took my paperwork, and said that I needed to have my wife present. I gave her the reason why that was impossible, and pointed out my carefully written explanation. She gave me a number and told me to have a seat, whence the clock started ticking in earnest. I needed to be out of there by 2:00 in order to make it back to Newark Airport by 4:00 or all would be lost. It was a Friday and if we missed that flight, there wasn't another one until Monday, which would be too late to bother taking the trip at all. My heart rate continued upward despite no exercise being undertaken. Homeland Security guards watched my restless kids who were squirming on the floor and crawling all over me, jockeying for lap space. Something needed to be done about their energy or we'd get thrown out. I ordered them to start walking laps in circular route around that big room.

It took an hour before I was called to another window. Another official said that the excuse I offered for my wife's lack of visibility was insufficient. I would need a notarized letter from Wife certifying her agreement to issue the kids' passports to me. I explained that she was in a tiny town in Italy, many time zones into the future, and that procuring such a document might be impossible. "I'll let you speak to my supervisor," he says, "but she'll tell you the same thing I did, only in different words." Before he could even finish, his superior was already standing behind her man, surveying us with gimlet eyes. She looked at Boy, his face covered with welts. She glanced over at Girl, whose throw-up stained clothes highlighted her pale greenish color. Never before have two kids looked more like they were being abducted and hustled out of the country by a crazed father. The supervisor, an employee of the U.S. State Dept. said, "you mean to tell me that there isn't a single fax machine in the entire town of Italy?" At this point, I could no longer contain my impulse to speak the truth. "It's a country," I said, doing my best to hide my exasperation. "And it's not a good enough reason either," she shot back. I was handed a list of local fax offices and advised to return with the requisite document. We dashed out the door to the nearest one, got their incoming fax number, and relayed it to Wife on the other side of the world.

She called back an hour later with bad news. In Italy, they won't notarize a letter that's headed out of the country without a court order, and of course, it was 4pm on a Friday and the courts were closed for the weekend. I said that Italy is famous as the land of lax officialdom, and to keep trying to find someone who'll notarize. The kids and I went back to wandering the streets of Philly awaiting either a call back from her, or for my cell phone batteries to die, whichever came first. Another hour ticked by. Then the call came to go to the fax office. I watched as a notarized letter was slowly emerging from the mountains of northern Italy. The magic was back. I grabbed the letter and raced back to the Customs House. The official inspected the letter carefully, gave me another number, and directed me to have a seat. I watched the clock ticking away as case after case got called to the window. The kids began acting half crazed and somehow manage to maintain that state for the next two hours while I tried to remain calm, waiting patiently, doing penance for my egregious error regarding that couch. At 1:00, they called me forth, asked my kids who's their daddy, made me swear an oath, and issued their passports.

We scrambled into the car and raced out of Philly with the knowledge that if I hit any traffic, made one wrong turn, or obeyed the speed limit, we'd miss the flight. But I-95 northbound smiled on us that day, and I pulled into Newark airport with seconds to spare before flight time. The gate ticket agent greeted me by saying, "sorry, the flight's overbooked. There are no seats for you." The whole surreal adventure had become like an action movie where the protagonist must overcome increasingly difficult obstacles. I wished I'd never set the whole escapade in motion by bringing home that damned couch.

We were placed on a waiting list and I sat down with the kids directly in front of the gate agent in order to be a persistent presence. An announcer began offering other passengers money to give up their seats, and when it reached $700, enough of them bailed and we got three tickets to Milan. Mission accomplished, or so I thought.`

I dragged the kids into the crush of people funneling up to the boarding gateway. We were in the thick of things when Girl suddenly took off running and disappeared into the sea of people behind us. Gone. I sprinted after her in a near panic with Boy in tow, dodging people while catching fleeting glimpses of a figure that might be her, dashing away from us at full speed through the packed terminal. Missing our flight had become the least of my worries. I had lost Girl at JFK airport.

I found her on the bench where we had been waiting for the flight. She had left her stuffed animal there was not about to fly across the ocean without it. I scooped both of them up and hustled back to the jetway just as they were closing the doors. A huge rush of relief, mixed with a sense of disbelief that we had actually made it, washed over me as we boarded the plane. But my trials were far from over.

Halfway through the flight, Girl had a nightmare from which she could not be awakened. She thrashed about, screaming at full volume, her red eyes glaring blankly. I struggled to keep her from running around the plane wild and asleep. She fought me for all she was worth. Then Boy got so ill that he couldn't move. For the first time, I understood the blank face that Buster Keaton had made famous. The whole exhausting ordeal had transformed me into a shell of a man, all hollowed out with nobody home, just like Buster. Then we landed in Milan.

Getting kids to a bathroom multiple times in a foreign airport while waiting for your baggage to hit the carousel is not a calming affair, especially when all the other passengers have collected their bags long ago, leaving you in a revolving hell of uncertainty. I was very grateful to have ours at all when they arrived an hour later, and to be walking out of that terminal toward the location of our rental car in the expansive parking lot beyond. Grateful and relieved, that is, until a frigid Alpine rainstorm suddenly cleared the nearby peaks and drenched us with icy torrents. We continued to make our way across the rain swept parking lot, but the rental car was nowhere to be found. I had to drag the kids back to the office, where they offered to drive me to the car, which, it turned out, was in a different lot altogether. I piled the wet and freezing kids inside, loaded the soggy luggage, and headed off to Verona, a mere 2 hours away, which sounds like an easy jaunt unless you don't speak the language and haven't slept in 48 hours. My first challenge was to get out of the parking lot, which I navigated thanks to the blaring horns and gestures of other drivers prompting me like an Italian default guidance system. I managed to find my way out and onto the Autostrada, only to be met by more blinding rain and heavy truck traffic that had turned this stretch of Mussolini's dream into a nightmare. Both kids were fast asleep in the back, and the only things keeping me awake were the waves of water thrown up by the oncoming traffic that hit my windshield like hard slaps in the face, and the scary drifting of our Lancia as it hydroplaned eastward across the country.

One pictures Verona as a sleepy little hill town where Juliet swooned from her balcony. In reality, it's a busy maze ringed by industrial flats that are impenetrable unless you're a native Veronese. Had I not been armed with a GPS that was the only English language speaker for miles around, we would have certainly spent the night in the rental car parked illegally in the lot of a factory or a strip mall outside town. It felt like the miracle of San Gennaro when I found the rental apartment complex hidden deep within the inner city. Despite my confirmed reservations, the people at the front desk were not expecting us. I guess they figured we'd get lost, give up searching, and check in wherever we could, leaving our prepaid room with them open for other paying guests. What they couldn't figure out was why I was the happiest guest they had ever tried to swindle. Mine was the laugh of a mad man, and this display of good cheer unnerved them to such a degree that we were handed a room key immediately. Everyone piled into the elevator. When it opened at our floor, I was surprised to find no hallway, just a landing on a metal stairwell that was totally enclosed in cinderblock. We hauled out the luggage, the elevator door closed, and then everything went pitch black. Knowing that the steep metal stairs loomed within a few feet, I envisage the worst: the kids would take a step in the wrong direction and tumble down to their deaths. "Don't move!" I yell to them, as a final burst of adrenaline rushed through my battered brain. I began feeling my way along the wall toward the only thing visible in the darkness, a tiny red dot. The highlight of my entire trip to Italy was finding out that it was a light switch, timed to turn off automatically as soon as any Americans came within its sight.

Boy and I reckoned that our Italian job took 15 years off of my life, give or take a few months. I had aged so visibly closer to death during the trip that he said he wanted me to send him a postcard from heaven, "one of those kinds with a little picture on it, so I'll know what it's like." Better yet, I say, I'll show you what it's like in your dreams. Done deal. He added one more request. "I want you to be there to guide me, you know, into heaven." Agreed, sight unseen. Being a SAHD or a MAHD is the adventure of a lifetime, and perhaps, thereafter.

Things Fall Apart

We have come to the most exasperating point in our little adventure. The experience of utter and complete vexation is not a singularity on this job—it is a thousand points of darkness that add up to the mother of all depressions. You might cast an eye around your kingdom one day, and find tumbleweeds of dog hair rolling across the hardwood prairie. Books of all shapes and sizes will litter all the floors. Broken windows? Goes without saying. Carved up furniture? What else is it good for, really? Furniture gnawed up? Tasty! Paint smacked off moldings, walls, and ceilings just to see it fly? Wonderful fun! After spending my days cleaning up unnecessary messes and fixing broken stuff over and over again, chaos has gained the upper hand. They get dressed only under extreme duress and physical intervention. Breakfast follies with the usual food dumps and faces smeared with goo are followed by kids up on counters making ape-like noises, all to a soundtrack of miserable crying. Entropy is not an abstract theory to anyone who's caring for multiple kids. Things fall apart continually over the course of several years no matter what you do, and you come to appreciate the close filial relationship between exasperation and depression. Sustained, skull-numbing bouts with tiny terrorists of love have left me knowing exactly how Mohammed Ali feels after a lifetime of headshots. Motherhood, I now see, is a kind of affliction. By enjoining their labors, I have come to understand and empathize with their plight.

The birth of your first child is truly one of the most thrilling experiences you will have on this plane of existence, and following a period of settling in, the aftermath will feel quite manageable. When the second one comes along, and has been around for awhile, you will begin to wonder, *am I going to survive this?* They will test you beyond your patience, beyond your physical and mental endurance, and yes, if you're unlucky, beyond the point at which you go stark raving mad. You will come to understand why mothers make the most lovable murderers. You will realize that when fathers snap, we opt for beating our wives and kids in drunken frenzies, but when moms snap, they simply eliminate the specific irritants. Let's get this crucial difference between moms and dads straight right now. We're constantly hearing all about abusive fathers, because their children live to tell the tale. We don't hear anything from children of abusive mothers because, well, they're dead.

The happy entry you're reading was precipitated by that joyous holiday on the Christian calendar whereby we are all directed to go out and spend money like drunken sailors. As usual, the kids and I cut our own tree at the farm, then hauled it home and decorated it in the living room. For safety's sake, we hung only plastic ornaments, but somehow a glass one slipped through, and of course it was the only one that dropped, shattering into a hundred razor sharp slivers on the floor underneath bare, tender feet. I carried the kids out of the room, cleaned up the hazardous mess, and then took a short break in the kitchen, which the kids took as an opportunity to return stealthily on a mission to un-decorate the tree. I got there as Boy was pulling off the last of the lights. Decorating a tree once can be done with good spirits, but do it twice and evil ones begin to creep into the process. Afterwards, we went straight to bed, exhausted one and all. Then at 3:30am in the morning, the biggest, loudest, smashingest sound I have ever heard came from downstairs. The seven-foot Douglas fir tree had crashed to the floor, spreading the decorations, lights, and water from the base over the entire living room. It had become unbalanced by the attentions of harassing Liliputians, and much like myself, it was in pieces on the floor.

The world must realize that when a mother gets depressed, it's often a normal reaction to her seemingly impossible situation. Real healing would require society to make a seismic shift toward providing her with support that properly values children and the people who care for them. Instead, we find it cheaper, more convenient, and most importantly, much more profitable to medicate her. Just Zombie that Mother out! Make sure that she keeps needing your little pills by marginalizing her and mocking her social standing. Eliminate the old and oddly effective therapy of sitting on park benches and complaining, and replace it with happy doings on that Nexus of Narcissism, Facebook, which will only magnify her sense of dislocation. Or better yet, we'll cunningly offer another way out: be more like us men, dammit, and get thee to an office! Kneel before me and I'll pay you 70% of what I'd pay a similarly qualified man. Forget that stuff about child-raising! It's for sissies. Real women have jobs, and they outsource the rest. Don't like it? Take a look at all the depressed, impoverished mothers out there. You don't want to be like them, do you? Become a "working mother." I love that one. It says that the work of raising children isn't work, really. More word magic! We are brilliant, no? After all, if you don't use your smarts for manipulation, what good are they? Now you can have kids AND a boss. Get dissed at home and at the office! Then we wonder, what's wrong with Alice? We saved her from being a Mad Housewife and gave her the best of both worlds. She's the lucky juggler who's got it all.

The frustration of this predicament was recently articulated by my wife, who spent a Thanksgiving weekend with the kids in closer proximity than ever before. After cleaning up the fifth mess created by Girl for apparently no other reason than to see it get cleaned up, Wife snapped. "That's time you took from me that I can never get back! Do you understand?" I stood by in amusement thinking that, yes, I for one do understand, and for once she and I understood each other, but the kid had no idea what she was talking about.

If you're on the job, the day will come when you'll swear that the whole undertaking is specially designed to drive you crazy. You will become vexed when you discover that simply requesting a kid something, or to not do something, either of which usually refers to the protection of life, limb, or property, will be wholly inadequate to achieving the clearly stated ends. In the good old days, much was cured by short, simple spankings now and then. Of course, that's the modern day shibboleth, but spanking's fall from popularity is not why I refrain from indulging in it. I do so because my son pointed out that when kids are little, their will is strong but their minds and bodies are weak. Then, when they get older, their minds and bodies are strong, but their will has gotten weak. The answer to why I do not spank is in there, somewhere. You go figure it out. A tougher question is whether it is within my rights to use my voice like a bullhorn. Do you have kids? Do you have a pulse? Then you have, too. And if you haven't, it's probably because you're one of those people who will explode one day and kill them all in a blind rage. I'm not saying that you should yell. I'm just that you should not kill your kids.

My sister says it takes 4 years to recover from having a child, but at what age does the clock start ticking down? I say it starts after they've dropped the tantrums at around 5 years of age. Therefore, having one child means that it will take you almost a decade to return to normal. If you have two kids spaced 3 years apart, it will take 12 years, and so on. (I wrote those estimates years ago, but only now have I had the chance to transcribe it, and guess how old Boy is? Yes, he's 12.). A lot of stuff will get broken in the interim. Pray that you are not among them. I confess that this job may be more than I can handle, which brings up the main problem with men taking over this job: they might crumble physically, mentally, and spiritually under the load. Boy saw that I was approaching that point recently, and he asked me if I would be happier if they ran away. I didn't have the heart to tell him that it's the Dads who usually run away.

The Divine Comedy

Like Dante, I awoke one day in midlife and found myself lost in a dark wood. Things had become hazy, as though I were living through a near-death experience. Yet Dante knew that moments of supreme stress often bring on mystical visions during which you glimpse the truth behind everyday reality. Limbo is a grocery store crammed with dazed mothers wandering the aisles with fixed, thousand mile stares. Purgatory is the playground, where time crawls and you pay for the pleasures of sex in servitude to the beings who sprang from those very pleasures. Would these pitiable souls have indulged in those pleasurable moments if they had known it would translate into hours, days, nay, years parked in playgrounds? Yet, they are caught in the cosmic paradox of praying with all their might for the continuance of the little lives that are causing their servitude. Hell, on the other hand, is a simple place, a place to which I devoted an earlier chapter. It's having a kid disappear without a trace. Just one glimpse of it—as in the case of Eton Patz--forever changed the way that children are raised all across America. Luckily, yours' will almost definitely reappear, but the experience, however brief, will leave an indelible mark upon your soul. Heaven is equally simple. It is seeing your kid helping someone, usually another kid, who's having a hard time.

Yet another paradox of this job is that you can only slay your dragons by surrendering—surrendering your old identity so that a new one can emerge. Sometimes help comes in the form of a healing dream, or a jarring one, that ushers you across this threshold. Which brings us to my Einsteinian breakthrough, the point of this book and of your life. I call it the Special Theory of Generativity. Poor old Uncle Albert couldn't see the grand unified principle that eluded him all his life because he was never on the job. The most fundamental law of the universe is Generativity. The cosmos is forever bringing forth. You can either ride that tiger, or curl up with your device and imagine that you've got a life. Boy once asked me, "what's the difference between salvation and redemption?" In the end, nothing, because what you're left with is the same: a new level of consciousness, arrived at through personal sacrifice. We generate children and they regenerate us. The only questions that now remains in the world of physics are: why, God, did you make rubber bands so delicious, if you don't play dice with the universe, why, do you let kids eat them? There might be one last question that I'd like to ask the Gini: how heavy does a 35 pound sack of squirming, battling protoplasm become when carried out of a bed, stuffed into clothes, hefted down two flight of stairs, buckled into a car seat, then out of a car seat, carried 200 yards through a park, and then back through all these steps, entirely against it's own will? The number is beyond simple calculation, I assure you. Try it sometime and ponder the mystery.

And so, caring for children will drive you to the edge of your sanity, and either you break on through to the other side, or you go by the wayside. Kids can help you walk the line between a state of rationality and control so stultifying that your imagination gets snuffed out, and the kind of chaos that ensues when an Iranian high-speed centrifuge gets commandeered by a virus engineered by the Mosad. If you can harness the dance of Chaos and Control, you could become an avant-garde artist, a theoretical physicist, your own guru, Agent 86, or even an honest to goodness happy SAHD.

Unwrapping the Present

We all continually move on the edges of eternity, and are sometimes granted vistas through the fabric of illusion.

Ansel Adams

Children are little Zen masters who don't intend to be Zen masters, which makes them authentically Zen-like. They live strictly in the present moment, and they want you to join them in the here and now. They'll pull you away from whatever you're doing, no matter how important you think it might be, and force you to pay attention to the possibilities of the moment. Whereas a grownup Zen master might hit you with a stick to bring your attention back to the present, a child will achieve the same end by making a terrible mess either in the physical realm, or in the mental realm by trashing all of your plans. You can either let anger take over, or attend to the job at hand. They will test you thus daily. You will backslide, then make some progress, only to have your limits tested at a higher level. The Zen elves want you to practice the kind of awareness that requires a complete change in your state of mind. They become the teachers and you become the student. Let your mind wander, and they'll cane you pretty quickly. Are you a superior man, or are you ruled by impulses and desires? I constantly struggle with this challenge, probably because I'm trying to write a book while raising them, which is one task too many.

We once asked Boy if he'd like to say something as grace before dinner. He was only three years old at the time, but he said it all in only four words: "thank you for time." Time is the original blessing—it's all we really have. Life is over in the blink of an eye, and when we're there, we'll say, "that was fun, even the difficult parts--especially the difficult parts. Can I do it again?" The fact that the answer is a big fat NO makes every moment, both the good and the bad, precious beyond words. Another paradox you will experience while on the job, perhaps the most profound one for you personally, is the process whereby kids renew you while also bringing you closer to death. You will age double-time while they are in your care, yet time itself will take on a new meaning. The timelessness of the here and now will become self-evident during those fleeting moments when an ethereal tableaux crystallizes before your eyes. They're like still lives, but real ones of fathomless depth, and they occur everyday no matter how grinding or stressful things might get. It's very easy to miss them amidst the total mess of mealtime, the cacophony of crying, the cleaning of messy poop, and the countless other tasks that keep you spinning. These still lives are impossible to describe, but I must try knowing that I will fail, Zen-like.

One day I collapsed onto the couch after the typical twelve-hour shift managing the food input/output system while continuously maintaining homeland security vigilance. Both kids clambered up onto me, with Boy coming to rest on top while Girl snuggled into my side, and they both fell fast asleep. With all those alpha waves tuning up my brain, and their little angelic faces within inches of mine, I found the next hour as relaxing as if I had crawled into a languorous Gauguin painting and taken a nap. No one needs to become a reclusive yogi to realize the cyclical, eternal nature of reality. Kids will happily show you the way.

Another time, 6 year-old Boy stood on a gigantic round rubber float on a lake high in the mountains of northern Vermont. We were alone, swimming in rainwater used to make snow for ski runs. Without any warning, he transformed the float into a huge drum, and began pounding out an intertribal beat that echoed off the surrounding peaks in syncopated rhythm. The sound seemed to belong there. It was as if he'd somehow rediscovered a spot used by Abenaki drummers centuries ago. He completed the musical homecoming when he began chanting along. Then he stopped, stood up, let out a Tarzan whoop, and plunged into the clear water teeming with fat tadpoles. Raising children is the act of singing songs of innocence, but the specifics are not for innocent ears.

As I write this line, another tableaux appeared. Boy led Girl away down the hall while a folk ballad played on the radio. She looked over her shoulder and waved goodbye to me. I glimpsed the larger sweep and saw that the whole thing will be unbearably poignant at the very end. In the meantime, making magic with children is the essence of a life well lived.

And so, the Zen practice of being a SAHD is a stripping away that fills you up, a flight of the imagination that keeps you grounded, an emptying out that lets you embrace the full sweep of existence. Those who have breakthroughs rather than breakdowns discover the first principle of Zen, which is that there is no Zen. With nothing to be attained, enlightenment is complete. Do you understand what I'm saying? Most likely, neither of us do—but the Zen elves sure do. Let children into your life, for real, and you have the chance to grow into a proper adult.

Unwrapping the present, then, is the whole key to parenthood. And when you unwrap the present, the gift you find inside is a reminder that life is a celebration. Kids know that the best possible way to live this short Earth Walk is in celebratory play. They want to celebrate every discovery, every event, and every moment, big time. The best you can do is to go ahead and celebrate with them, and playfully pursue the truth of being here and now. You've been given the gift of life. It's up to you to unwrap the present.

The Primary Love Object

From a kid's perspective, the adult who cares for you with their own hands matters more than anything else in the world, and the love they give you in return is beyond all reason. If you're the parent, (or the nanny!), who's put in the hours, days, and years into this process, then the die is cast and nothing can change it. Try as you might to pay lip service to your wife's need to feel like an equal partner in child-rearing decisions, the fact is that you're the boss who earns that title daily by also being the servant. The secret at the core of all family dynamics is that the heart of a child contains room for only one primary love object. Sure, they let others in, but only one person is allowed to hold the key, and if you're a genuine SAHD, then you are the key-holder.

After being on this job for a number of years, your kids won't just love you. They will love you crazy. Basking in the tractor beam of that love is the payback for all of your troubles. Maybe that's why there's no lucre in it. They pay billionaires their billions while keeping mothers at home in abject poverty, for they know that a child's love is beyond valuation. (Rosebud!). This gift of singular love gets thrown into high relief because it will not be given to your spouse in equal measure. Things here get most dicey for a SAHD, because how many mothers do you know are willing to hold second place in their kid's hearts?

My kids expect that my face will be the last one that they see at the night and the first one that they see in the morning. In between those moments, it will be my name that they call out from their sleep, looking for comfort from the anguish of nightmares. They look to me for cues on how to think about everything in the world from sex to death and back again. However unwittingly I got here, Wife feels bereft with me in the position of primary love object. She said that, "you never recognized how hard it is on me, to have a child run to you whenever they get hurt, even if I'm right next them. I'm a doctor, too, but they'll run to you even if you're on the other side of the house and leap into your arms." She claims it's simply because they imprinted on me, but would they have imprinted on me if I'd done a poor job? I was the one who walked them to school everyday, who visited their classrooms and went to teacher conferences, who fed them, bathed them, clothed them, and played with them for years on end. When you do that level of work, you earn a type of absolute trust and love that adults don't understand. Mothers who forfeit these tasks will also forfeit the preponderance of her kids' affection. They can't expect traditional roles to hold when it's convenient, and they might feel wounded by the fact that you're way more important in their lives. But the fact is that they cannot expect to get the same love and respect that you do. They cannot come home from their jobs and suddenly step into your role and take over. The kids will not allow it. Adjustments of the heart will have to be made, or the arrangement will not work out.

Men seem better suited to sitting in the backseat when it comes to their kids' affection. For women, it seems much harder to bear. My own mother was devastated by the fact that her mother-in-law supplanted her as her kids' primary love object. Our grandmother was on the job, making breakfast, lunch, and dinner, and hanging out with us every day. Mom was the ghost in the machine who did a thousand largely invisible jobs for the eleven people in our household, and hence sacrificed being in the pole position to receive her children's love. So do not try any of this at home, unless you have a wife who's willing to abdicate first place in her children's lives to you. And believe me, in those little hearts, there is no parity and no equality. There is only hierarchy. If you take this job, you shall stand at the pinnacle of that peak, but the price you must pay requires sacrifices too big for most men to make.

For most men, as indeed for me, caring for multiple children is the stunt of a lifetime. Forget playing monopoly capital in your industry of choice, or visiting the space station, or drawing accolades as a performer. These distractions are easy by comparison, with pay-offs measurable in dollars earned or public attention lavished upon you. On the other hand, the currency children use to pay you back is the only currency they have, which is the only currency worth a damn anyway. That's why women have done this job for eons. The species of love you receive doesn't require you to tell them that you love them back. It doesn't care that you've got all those flaws. It doesn't even recognize the possibility of the presence of other potential love objects out there. This kind of love should have a different name, so different is it from the varieties of love we are accustomed to receiving from other quarters. This love is stellar. It rocks your world, but only if you've put in the years, hands-on and day-to-day, with little hired help. Those of you in this category already know what I'm talking about. It's a transcendent, transporting tractor beam of emotion that hits you like the warmth of Hawaiian sunlight. In its presence, life and death fall into their rightful, secondary place. This is the love of the infinite. The possibility of being on the receiving end of it is the reason you should try the job. There it is, the point of this book. The home fires have forged my new identity. Any project that I can imagine taking on is a feeble substitute for bathing in the distilled essence of love that the kids shower upon me every day. The payback for my sacrifice is incalculable and eternal.

It is All Over. It Has Just Begun.

I'm not necessarily a wiser man from the hapless chap who stepped into this cauldron a decade ago, even though I've aged double-time. One thing I am more aware of--as in a quantum leap more aware—is that mothers are gifted and besieged people. I'm also aware that some cultures, which we call primitive, carry the belief that children are brought into this world by the dreams of their fathers. (I wrote that line long before somebody named Obama used it for a book title). The nice thing about that fanciful idea is that it gives fathers a special responsibility for their offspring. So dream well. Your kids are the greatest acts of creation that you will ever achieve, perhaps because they are not truly yours'. They belong to the great mystery, or whatever you want to call it. Through our kids, we work in partnership with the universe to help shape the future. So there should be no hurry in the task.

Before children, I never considered patience to be a virtue since it doesn't make or do anything, and so I had almost none. I was a young man in a hurry. When children showed up asking for food and fun, I realized that patience makes time, and time makes everything else. It is therefore the mother of all the other talents. Throughout the history of humankind, more food was produced by the archetypically feminine approach of snares and patience, than by the archetypically masculine approach of chasing and piercing. You can set a trap for a work of art, or an invention, or a scientific breakthrough, or a book. Set up the right conditions and it will come to you. It will wander by, drawn by the attractive smells of the tools of creation sitting ready. The finished products seem to be preexisting. They just want to find a home in the visible world. Kids can teach you this practice, if you let them.

Children can also be the storm surge that washes away your vanity, stupidity, survival mechanisms, fear of death, and all the other blunt instruments of an adult mind narrowed by living in our crazy culture. Their nonsensical talking, their improvised games, their pointless revelry can transport you further than any spacecraft yet invented. Raising children is an exploration into the Law of Paradoxes, and as such, it's the ultimate philosophical adventure, one that in the end leads you back home. My kids gave me everything, but first they took everything away. Go forth and raise them, and they shall raise you.

False Endings

I'm back because I was wrong, once again. Being wrong has become one of my greatest pleasures. The job doesn't end neatly. There are no nice tidy wrap-ups like the ones required for every Hollywood movie. With the blessings of the Almighty, it goes on until the roles are reversed and your kids are changing your diapers. I'm not even at the high school years yet, so who am I fooling? Not them. If having children—no—the experience of raising children day-in and day-out over a period of years has taught me one thing, it is that you will end up thinking big thoughts about ways to protect and improve the lives of all children. That's the true job of a Baby Wrestler.

Here in my house, we've reached the point where nearly all of the scatological mountaintops have been scaled. Food and drink stay in their places on the table. School attendance and homework have been accepted as inevitable but endurable tortures. Bad behaviors exhibited by their friends are no longer immediately mimicked and incorporated into habit. A weary truce is gradually descending upon the two of them as their fighting has begun to wane, though battles still flare up. One would think one is over the hump. Think again. "How is the Baby Wrestler going?" Boy asked. "Slow" I said. "Of course. Kids grow up slow," he replied, right again.

I look around now, so many years after starting this job, and see many other men not only doing the job, but doing it better than I could ever dream of doing it. All I really know is that with women rising in the work force, your chances of begin able to stay home with the kids has never been better. Now please excuse me while I go find out who the dog is trying to eat in the front yard, get my older kid off of YouTube, stop my younger one from overdosing on stevia, and get a job digging ditches.

Wrestle on!

Made in the USA
Charleston, SC
17 May 2014